Men Who Dared

by Barbara Jurgensen

Paraphrase by
Kenneth N. Taylor

A modern retelling of the lives and messages of the Minor Prophets

36

Tyndale House, Publishers
Wheaton, Illinois

Contents

*The Minor Prophets—oh, they're
the guys with the funny names at the end
of the Old Testament*

*I can't tell you much about
the Minor Prophets except for Jonah . . .
I know a little about him*

Who Were The Prophets?

THE PROPHETS WERE MEN.
>Not angels.
>Not supermen.
>Not some strange kind of creature.
>Men.

Men who dared, in the midst of a disinterested and hostile world, to stand up and speak for God.

Men who uttered God's words as He gave them, regardless of popular opinion, regardless of the threat to their own lives.

Men who lived God's way in troubled and difficult times, loving God and man.

The secret of their endurance and courage? They knew God.

For them God was not some shadowy, faraway, unknowable being. He was knowable and near. He was as real as they themselves.

They knew Him not only from their study of the sacred books, they had gone on to know Him personally, thinking about His Word and talking to Him as they went about their daily lives.

They stood in awe of Him as their realization grew day by day as to who and what He was.

The prophets were men. Men endowed with the same wonderful potential that the rest of us are endowed with—the potential of becoming faithful sons of God.

The prophets were not men who just went around predicting what was going to happen. They did that, but also much more. They brought the message of God to man. They tried to lead man back to God. They taught man to know God.

Their prophecies usually concerned what was going to happen *if* the people did not turn from their evil ways. Often the people listened to the words of the prophets and changed their ways; then the predicted disasters did not need to happen.

Each prophet was different. Each had his own personality. Some were married and had families to support.

For most of them, prophesying was something that they did in addition to their regular work. It was payment enough to them that God had chosen them as a means of speaking to His people.

And so they went and declared God's words to the people.

Each prophet had a particular message for the people of his time. The ideas about God that they put forth to the people may seem commonplace to us today, but we have the great advantage of the whole Bible revelation before us. And we, in our day, can learn wonderful truths from these prophets of other days.

The prophets also prepared the way for Jesus. Had Jesus been born in Athens or Rome, the people there probably would not have been ready to understand and receive Him and His teachings. But coming as He did into a situation where the prophets had gradually been leading the people into a more mature relationship with God, He found many who were eager and responsive.

Sometimes the prophets seem to be repeating each other unnecessarily. Actually the twelve minor prophets were strung out through history over a period of some four or five hundred years and lived in different parts of the country.

Hosea, Joel, Amos, Obadiah, Jonah, and Micah possibly lived in the 700's or 800's B.C.

Nahum, Habakkuk, and Zephaniah in the 600's B.C.

Haggai and Zechariah in the 500's B.C.

And Malachi in the 400's B.C. Roughly, the order in which the books appear in the Bible is possibly the order in which the various prophets lived.

God called the prophets into service whenever the people had slipped so far away from Him that He needed to use some direct means of calling them back.

The minor prophets were first so named by St. Augustine in the second century because their books are shorter than those of

Isaiah, Jeremiah, Ezekiel, and Daniel—whom he gave the name "major prophets."

The Hebrew prophets are unique among the prophets of the world.

The oracles at Delphi,

The readers of animal entrails in Mesopotamia,

And the augurs in Rome made claims of foretelling the future, but only the Hebrew prophets claimed to speak the will of God.

The Hebrew prophets alone attempted to answer the riddle of life by showing man what his relationship to God and man could and should be.

They showed the devastating effect of sin on one's own and one's nation's life, but they did not leave their hearers here. They showed also that, as man lives his life in a relationship of love to God and to man, life becomes not only bearable, but meaningful and satisfying.

If these men, these prophets, were able to accomplish so much, why doesn't God send us prophets today?

Perhaps because when He sent Christ to us, He gave us His full and complete word. In Christ He said and did all that needed to be said and done for man to be able to enter into the relationship God planned for him with those around him, with life itself, and with God.

Perhaps because He expects that each one who has become His son will become a bearer of His message to those around him.

Perhaps the prophets have been superseded by each person today who dares to live God's way.

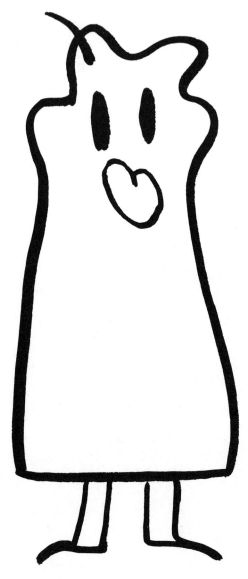

The Minor Prophets had some
weird ideas . . . I think.
Of course, I haven't read them . . .

Hosea's Weird Marriage

Hosea, the bachelor prophet, lived a peaceful existence, each day much like the one before it and the one after it, nothing spectacular ever happening to him. Then one day God suddenly threw a bombshell into his life. Out of the blue, God pitched him a weird assignment: *Go and marry a girl who is a prostitute.**

A prostitute! A woman who, instead of marrying one man and living with him, slept first with one man, then with others, ignoring God's commandment about adultery!

Hosea couldn't believe he was hearing right!

In the first place, he wasn't sure he wanted to get married at all. But to be joined in marriage—he, a servant of God—with a prostitute? He couldn't imagine such a thing! What was God trying to do?

God explained: He knew He had to do something drastic to show His people, the children of Israel, that they were playing the harlot to Him. Lately they had completely turned their backs on Him and practicing all sorts of wickedness and worshiping Baal. No longer did they even come into His holy temple; instead they flocked to tree-topped hills and bowed down to idols.

The people of Hosea's day weren't much different from us today. Things were so good, they had so much more than they needed, that they thought they could ignore God and their covenant with Him. During the hard years, when they'd been traveling from Egypt to their promised land, they had depended on God directly each day for all their needs—food, water, even

*Some Bible expositors say that Hosea may have married a woman he assumed was pure and discovered later she was unfaithful.

11

directions for the day's travel. But when they reached their rich land, it became easy to think of themselves as self-sufficient. They didn't realize that they still needed God. They hadn't caught on to the truth that man does not live by bread alone.

And God longed for the day when they would return to Him.

So Hosea went and married Gomer, a prostitute, and she bore him a son. Hosea named him Jezreel as God had instructed, for God planned to punish Israel by letting it be defeated in the valley called Jezreel.

When Gomer presented Hosea with a daughter, the Lord told him to name her Not Pitied to show that God had lost His compassion for Israel. And when she had another son, God ordered Hosea to call him Not My People, explaining, "Israel is not Mine and I am not her God."

God could not let the Chosen People go on the way they were. If they could see their depravity and unfaithfulness acted out in Hosea's marriage, perhaps they would see how far they had fallen, and would return to God.

In this acting out, Hosea represented God, the faithful One; his wife, the unfaithful people of Israel who went lusting after other husbands (gods); and their children were the natural fruit of such a relationship—suffering, sorrow, and separation from God.

God let the lesson sink in. He now waited for His people to realize the symbolic meaning of Hosea's marriage. As a catalyst to speed their awakening, God made life hard for them; He caused the grain then growing in the fields to develop with no heads, and the people cried out for food.

He turned allied nations against the Israelites and let their enemies attack and kill many of them. When children were born, God let the children sicken and die. If prosperous times had wooed them away from Him, maybe tough times would lead them back.

God sat and watched, waiting for the day when these people who were not now His people would be called "sons of the living God," when they would turn from their evil ways to walk again in His ways. He promised that when they returned to Him, He would make their land flourish—their fields would bear much grain, their children would grow and be strong. They would once more be His favored people, and He would be their revered God.

Sometimes God has spoken to His people with a still, small voice, as He did with Elijah; sometimes from a burning bush, as to Moses; sometimes with a dramatic acting out of the utter unfaithfulness of His people, as in Hosea's offbeat marriage.

A strange assignment—to marry a prostitute. God could hardly have chosen a more dramatic method to open the eyes of his people.

Hosea

CHAPTER 1

THESE ARE THE MESSAGES from the Lord to Hosea, son of Beeri, during the reigns of these four kings of Judah:
Uzziah,
Jotham,
Ahaz, and
Hezekiah;
and one of the kings of Israel, Jeroboam, son of Joash.

2 Here is the first message:

The Lord said to Hosea, "Go and marry a girl who is a prostitute, so that some of her children will be born to you from other men. This will illustrate the way My people have been untrue to Me, committing open adultery against Me by worshiping other gods."

3-5 So Hosea married Gomer, daughter of Diblaim, and she conceived and bore him a son. And the Lord said, "Name the child Jezreel, for in the Valley of Jezreel I am about to punish King Jehu's dynasty to avenge the murders[1] he committed; in fact, I will put an end to Israel as an independent kingdom, breaking the power of the nation in the Valley of Jezreel."[2]

6-7 Soon Gomer had another child—this one a daughter. And God said to Hosea, "Name her Lo-Ruhamah (meaning 'no more mercy') for I will have no more mercy upon Israel, to forgive her again. But I *will* have mercy on the tribe of Judah. I will personally free her from her enemies without any help from her armies or her weapons."[3]

8-11 After Gomer had weaned Lo-Ruhamah, she again conceived and this time gave birth to a son. And God said, "Call him Lo-Ammi (meaning 'not mine'), for Israel is not Mine and I am not her God. Yet the time will come when Israel shall prosper

[1]He went far beyond God's command to execute the family of Ahab. See 1 Kings 21:21 and 2 Kings 10:11.
[2]A prediction of the Assyrian conquest of Israel 25 years later.
[3]Soon after defeating Israel, the Assyrian Emperor Sennacherib invaded Judah and beseiged Jerusalem. He was driven off by special intervention of God's angel (Isaiah 37:36).

14

and become a great nation; in that day her people will be too numerous to count—like sand along a seashore! Then, instead of saying to them, 'You are not My people,' I will tell them, 'You are My sons, children of the Living God.' Then the people of Judah and Israel will unite and have one leader; they will return from exile together; what a day that will be—the day when God will sow His people in the fertile soil of their own land again.[4]

CHAPTER 2

O JEZREEL,[1] RENAME YOUR BROTHER AND SISTER. Call your brother Ammi (which means "Now you are mine"); name your sister Ruhamah ("Pitied"), for now God will have mercy upon her!

2-4 Plead with your mother; for she has become another man's wife—I am no longer her husband. Beg her to stop being a prostitute, to quit giving herself to others. If she doesn't, I will strip her as naked as the day she was born, and cause her to waste away and die of thirst as in a land riddled with famine and drought. And I will not give special favors to her children as I would to my own, for they are not my children; they belong to other men.

5-7 For their mother has committed adultery. She did a shameful thing when she said, "I'll run after other men and sell myself to them for food and drinks and clothes." But I will fence her in with briars and thornbushes; I'll block the road before her to make her lose her way, so that when she runs after her lovers she will not catch up with them. She will search for them but not find them. Then she will think, "I might as well return to my husband, for I was better off with Him than I am now."

8-9 She doesn't realize that all she has, has come from Me. It was I who gave her all the gold and silver with which she worshiped Baal, her god! But now I will take back the wine and ripened corn I constantly supplied, and the clothes I gave her to cover her nakedness—I will no longer give her rich harvests of grain in its season, or wine at the time of the grape harvest.

10-13 Now I will expose her nakedness in public for all her lovers to see, and no one will be able to rescue her from My hand. I will put an end to all her joys, her parties, holidays and

[4]Literally, "the day of Jezreel ('God Sows')" see 2:23.
[1]"Jezreel" is implied from the preceding chapter and verse.

15

feasts. I will destroy her vineyards and her orchards—gifts she claims her lovers gave her—and let them grow into a jungle; wild animals will eat their fruit. For all the incense that she burned to Baal her idol and for the times when she put on her earrings and jewels and went out looking for her lovers, and deserted Me: for all these things I will punish her," says the Lord.

14-16 But I will court her again, and bring her into the wilderness, and speak to her tenderly there. There I will give back her vineyards to her, and transform her Valley of Troubles into a Door of Hope. She will respond to me there, singing with joy as in days long ago in her youth, after I had freed her from captivity in Egypt. In that coming day, says the Lord, she will call me "My Husband" instead of "My Master."[2]

17-20 O Israel, I will cause you to forget your idols, and their names will not be spoken anymore. At that time 1 will make a treaty between you and the wild animals, birds and snakes, not to fear each other any more; and I will destroy all weapons, and all wars will end. Then you will lie down in peace and safety, unafraid; and I will bind you to Me forever with chains of righteousness and justice and love and mercy. I will betroth you to Me in faithfulness and love, and you will really know Me then as you never have before.

21-22 In that day, says the Lord, I will answer the pleading of the sky for clouds, to pour down water on the earth in answer to its cry for rain. Then the earth can answer the parched cry of the grain, the grapes, and the olive trees for moisture and for dew—and the whole grand chorus shall sing together that "God sows!"[3] He has given all!

23 At that time I will sow a crop of Israelites and raise them for Myself! I will pity those who are "not pitied,"[4] and I will say to those who are "not My people," "Now you are My people"; and they will reply, "You are our God!"

CHAPTER 3

THEN THE LORD SAID TO ME, "Go, and get your wife again and bring her back to you and love her, even though she loves adultery. For the Lord still loves Israel though she has turned to other gods and offered them choice gifts."

[2]Literally, "my Baal," meaning "my Lord," but this was a tainted word because applied to idols, so it will no longer be used in reference to the true God.
[3]Literally, "Jezreel."
[4]See chapter 1, verses 6, 9, and 10.

2-4 So I bought her (back from her slavery),[1] for a couple of dollars and eight bushels of barley, and I said to her, "You must live alone for many days; do not go out with other men nor be a prostitute; and I will wait for you." This illustrates the fact that Israel will be a long time without a king or prince; and without an altar, temple, priests, or even idols!

5 Afterwards they will return to the Lord their God, and to the Messiah, their king;[2] and they shall come trembling, submissive to the Lord and to His blessings, in the end times.

CHAPTER 4

HEAR THE WORD OF THE LORD, O people of Israel. The Lord has filed a lawsuit against you listing the following charges: There is no faithfulness, no kindness, no knowledge of God in your land.

2-3 You swear and lie and kill and steal and commit adultery. There is violence everywhere, with one murder after another. That is why your land is not producing; it is filled with sadness, and all living things grow sick and die; the animals, the birds, and even the fish begin to disappear.

4-6 Don't point your finger at someone else, and try to pass the blame to him! Look, priest, I am pointing My finger at *you*. As a sentence for your crimes, you priests will stumble in broad daylight as well as in the night; and so will your false "prophets" too; and I will destroy your mother, Israel. My people are destroyed because they don't know Me; and it is all your fault, you priests, for you yourselves refuse to know Me; therefore I refuse to recognize you as My priests. Since you have forgotten My laws, I will "forget" to bless your children.

7 The more My people multiplied, the more they sinned against Me. They exchanged the glory of God for the disgrace of idols.

8-10 The priests rejoice in the sins of the people; they lap it up and lick their lips for more! And thus it is: "Like priest, like people"—because the priests are wicked, the people are too. Therefore, I will punish both priests and people for all their wicked deeds. They will eat and still be hungry. Though they do a big business as prostitutes, they shall have no children, for they have deserted Me and turned to other gods.

[1]Implied.
[2]Literally, "to David, their king." Christ was "the greater David."

17

11-13 Wine, women, and song have robbed My people of their brains. For they are asking a piece of wood to tell them what to do. "Divine Truth" comes to them through tea leaves![1] Longing after idols has made them foolish. For they have played the harlot, serving other gods, deserting Me. They sacrifice to idols on the tops of mountains; they go up into the hills to burn incense beneath the pleasant shade of oaks and poplars and terebinth trees. There your daughters turn to prostitution and your brides commit adultery.

14 But why should I punish them? For you men are doing the same thing, sinning with prostitutes and temple-girls. Fools! Your doom is sealed, for you refuse to understand.

15-17 But though Israel is a prostitute, may Judah stay far from such a life. O Judah, do not join with those who insincerely worship me at Gilgal and at Bethel. Their worship is a mere pretense. Don't be like Israel, stubborn as a heifer, resisting the Lord's attempts to lead her in green pastures. Stay away from her, for she is wedded to idolatry.

18-19 The men of Israel finish up their drinking bouts, and off they go to find some prostitutes. Their love for shame is greater than for honor.[2] Therefore, a mighty wind[3] shall sweep them away; they shall die in shame, because they sacrifice to idols.

CHAPTER 5

LISTEN TO THIS, you priests and all of Israel's leaders; listen, all you men of the royal family: You are doomed! For you have deluded the people with idols at Mizpah and Tabor,

2-4 And dug a deep pit to trap them at Acacia. But never forget—I will settle up with all of you for what you've done. I have seen your evil deeds: Israel, you have left Me as an adulteress does her husband; you are utterly defiled. Your deeds won't let you come to God again; for the spirit of adultery is deep within you, and you cannot know the Lord.

5 The very arrogance of Israel testifies against her in My court. She will stumble under her load of guilt, and Judah, too, shall fall.

[1]Literally, "their staff." There is no modern parallel to this ancient practice used by sorcerers, whose predictions were based on how their staffs landed on the ground when thrown or allowed to fall.
[2]The Hebrew text is uncertain. This translation follows the Greek version.
[3]The Assyrian invasion came about 20 years later and the nation disappeared.

6-7 Then at last they will come with their flocks and herds to sacrifice to God, but it will be too late—they will not find Him. He has withdrawn from them and they are left alone. For they have betrayed the honor of the Lord, bearing children that aren't His. Suddenly they and all their wealth will disappear.

8-9 Sound the alarm! Warn with trumpet blasts in Gibeah and Ramah, and on over to Bethaven; tremble, land of Benjamin! Hear this announcement, Israel: When your day of punishment comes, you will become a heap of rubble.

10-12 The leaders of Judah have become the lowest sort of thieves.[1] Therefore, I will pour My anger down upon them like a waterfall; and Ephraim will be crushed and broken by My sentence because she is determined to follow idols. I will destroy her as a moth does wool; I will sap away the strength of Judah like dry rot.

13-15 When Ephraim and Judah see how sick they are, Ephraim will turn to Assyria, to the great king there; but he can neither help nor cure. I will tear Ephraim and Judah as a lion rips apart its prey; I will carry them off and chase all rescuers away. I will abandon them and return to My home until they admit their guilt and look to Me for help again; for as soon as trouble comes, they will search for Me and say:

CHAPTER 6

COME, LET US RETURN TO THE LORD; it is He who has torn us—He will heal us. He has wounded—He will bind us up.

2-3 In just a couple of days,[2] or three at the most, He will set us on our feet again, to live in His kindness! Oh, that we might know the Lord! Let us press on to know Him, and He will respond to us as surely as the coming of dawn or the rain of early spring."

4-5 O Ephraim and Judah, what shall I do with you? For your love vanishes like morning clouds, and disappears like dew. I sent My prophets to warn you of your doom; I have slain you with the words of My mouth, threatening you with death. Suddenly, without warning, My judgment will strike you as surely as day follows night.

6-9 I don't want your sacrifices—I want your love; I don't

[1]Literally, "as those who move a boundary marker." See Deut. 19:14; 27:17.
[2]Literally, "In two days."

19

want your offerings—I want you to know Me. But like Adam, you broke My covenant; you refused My love. Gilead is a city of sinners, tracked with footprints of blood. Her citizens are gangs of robbers, lying in ambush for their victims; packs of priests murder along the road to Shechem and practice every kind of sin.

10-11 Yes, I have seen a horrible thing in Israel—Ephraim chasing other gods, Israel utterly defiled. O Judah, for you also there is a plentiful harvest of punishment waiting—and I wanted so much to bless you!

CHAPTER 7

I WANTED TO FORGIVE ISRAEL but her sins were far too great—no one can even live in Samaria without being a liar, thief and bandit!

2 Her people never seem to recognize that I am watching them. Their sinful deeds give them away on every side; I see them all.

3-4 The king is glad about their wickedness; the princes laugh about their lies. They are all adulterers; as a baker's oven is constantly aflame—except while he kneads the dough and waits for it to rise—so are these people constantly aflame with lust.

5-8 On the king's birthday, the princes get him drunk; he makes a fool of himself and drinks with those who mock him. Their hearts blaze like a furnace with intrigue. Their plot smolders through the night, and in the morning it flames forth like raging fire. They kill their kings one after another,[1] and none cries out to Me for help. My people mingle with the heathen, picking up their evil ways; thus they become as good-for-nothing as a half-baked cake!

9-10 Worshiping foreign gods has sapped their strength, but they don't know it. Ephraim's hair is turning gray, and he doesn't even realize how weak and old he is. His pride in other gods has openly condemned him; yet he doesn't return to his God, nor even try to find Him.

11-13 Ephraim is a silly, witless dove, calling to Egypt, flying to Assyria. But as she flies, I throw My net over her and bring her down like a bird from the sky; I will punish her for all her evil ways. Woe to My people for deserting Me; let them perish, for they have sinned against Me. I wanted to redeem them but their

[1]Three Israelite kings were assassinated during Hosea's lifetime—Zechariah, Shallum and Pekahiah.

hard hearts would not accept the truth.

14 They lie there sleepless with anxiety, but won't ask My help. Instead, they worship heathen gods, asking them for crops and for prosperity.

15-16 I have helped them, and made them strong; yet now they turn against Me. They look everywhere except to heaven, to the God above all gods. They are like a crooked bow that always misses its targets; their leaders will perish by the sword of the enemy for their insolence to Me. And all Egypt will laugh at them.

CHAPTER 8

SOUND THE ALARM! They are coming! Like a vulture, the enemy descends upon the people of God because they have broken My treaty and revolted against My laws.

2-4 Now Israel pleads with Me and says, "Help us, for You are our God!" But it is too late! Israel has thrown away her chance disdainfully, and now her enemies will chase her. She has appointed kings and princes, but not with My consent. They have cut themselves off from My help by worshiping the idols that they made from their silver and gold.

5-6 O Samaria, I reject this calf—this idol you have made. My fury burns against you. How long will it be before one honest man is found among you? When will you admit this calf you worship was made by human hands! It is not God! Therefore, it must be smashed to bits.

7-10 They have sown the wind and they will reap the whirlwind. Their cornstalks stand there barren, withered, sickly, with no grain; if it has any, foreigners will eat it. Israel is destroyed; she lies among the nations as a broken pot. She is a lonely, wandering wild ass. The only friends she has are those she hires; Assyria is one of them. But though she hires "friends" from many lands, I will send her off to exile. Then for a while at least she will be free of the burden of her wonderful king!

11-14 Ephraim has built many altars, but they are not to worship Me! They are altars of sin! Even if I gave her ten thousand laws, she'd say they weren't for her—that they applied to someone far away. Her people love the ritual of their sacrifice, but to Me it is meaningless! I will call for an accounting of their sins and punish them; they shall return to Egypt. Israel has built great palaces; Judah has constructed great defenses for her cities; but they have forgotten their Maker. Therefore, I will send down fire upon those palaces and burn those fortresses.

CHAPTER 9

O ISRAEL, REJOICE NO MORE AS OTHERS DO, for you have deserted your God and sacrificed to other gods on every threshing floor.

2 Therefore your harvests will be small; your grapes will blight upon the vine.

3-6 You may no longer stay here in this land of God; you will be carried off to Egypt and Assyria, and live there on scraps of food. There far from home, you are not allowed to pour out wine for sacrifice to God. For no sacrifice that is offered there can please Him; it is polluted, just as food of mourners is; all who eat such sacrifices are defiled. They may eat this food to feed themselves, but may not offer it to God. What then will you do on holy days, on days of feasting to the Lord, when you are carried off to Assyria as slaves? Who will inherit your possessions left behind? Egypt will! She will gather your dead; Memphis will bury them. And thorns and thistles will grow up among the ruins.

7-9 The time of Israel's punishment has come; the day of recompense is almost here and soon Israel will know it all too well. "The prophets are crazy"; "The inspired men are mad." Yes, so the people mock, for the nation is weighted with sin, and shows only hatred for those who love God. I appointed the prophets to guard My people, but the people have blocked them at every turn and publicly declared their hatred, even in the Temple of the Lord. The things My people do are as depraved as what they did in Gibeah[1] long ago. The Lord does not forget. He will surely punish them.

10 O Israel, how well I remember those first delightful days when I led you through the wilderness! How refreshing was your love! How satisfying, like the early figs of summer in their first season! But then you deserted Me for Baal-peor,[2] to give yourselves to other gods, and soon you were as foul as they.

11-12 The glory of Israel flies away like a bird, for your children will die at birth, or perish in the womb, or never even

[1]See Judges, chapter 9.
[2]Baal-peor, the god of Peor, a city of Moab. See Numbers, chapter 23.

be conceived. And if your children grow, I will take them from you; all are doomed. Yes, it will be a sad day when I turn away and leave you alone.

13-14   In my vision I have seen the sons of Israel doomed. The fathers are forced to lead their sons to slaughter. O Lord, what shall I ask for Your people? I will ask for wombs that don't give birth; for breasts that cannot nourish.

15-17   All their wickedness began at Gilgal;[3] there I began to hate them. I will drive them from My land because of their idolatry. I will love them no more, for all their leaders are rebels. Ephraim is doomed. The roots of Israel are dried up; she shall bear no more fruit. And if she gives birth, I will slay even her beloved child. My God will destroy the people of Israel because they will not listen or obey.

They will be wandering Jews, homeless among the nations.

CHAPTER 10

How PROSPEROUS ISRAEL IS—a luxuriant vine all filled with fruit! But the more wealth I give her, the more she pours it on the altars of her heathen gods; the richer the harvests I give her, the more beautiful the statues and idols she erects.

2-4   The hearts of her people are false toward God. They are guilty and must be punished. God will break down their heathen altars and smash their idols. Then they will say, "We deserted the Lord and He took away our king. But what's the difference? We don't need one anyway!" They make promises they don't intend to keep. Therefore punishment will spring up among them like poisonous weeds in the furrows of the field.

5-8   The people of Samaria tremble lest their calf-god idols at Bethaven should be hurt; the priests and people, too, mourn over the departed honor of their shattered gods. This idol—this calf-god thing—will be carted with them when they go as slaves to Assyria, a present to the great king there. Ephraim will be laughed at for trusting in this idol; Israel will be put to shame. As for Samaria, her king shall disappear like a chip of wood upon an ocean wave. And the idol altars of Aven at Bethel where Israel sinned will crumble. Thorns and thistles will grow up to surround them. And the people will cry to the mountains and hills to fall upon them and crush them.

---

[3]Gilgal: the town where Baal-worship flourished (Hosea 4:15; 12:11), and where the monarchy, hated of God, was instituted. (I Samuel 11:15).

9-10 O Israel, ever since that awful night in Gibeah,* there has been only sin, sin, sin! You have made no progress whatever. Was it not right that the men of Gibeah were wiped out? I will come against you for your disobedience; I will gather the armies of the nations against you to punish you for your heaped up sins.

11 Ephraim is accustomed to treading out the grain—an easy job she loves; I have never put her under a heavy yoke before; I have spared her tender neck. But now I will harness her to the plow and harrow. Her days of ease are gone.

12 Plant the good seeds of righteousness and you will reap a crop of My love; plow the hard ground of your hearts, for now is the time to seek the Lord, that He may come and shower salvation upon you.

13-15 But you have cultivated wickedness and raised a thriving crop of sins. You have earned the full reward of trusting in a lie—believing that military might and great armies can make a nation safe! Therefore the terrors of war shall rise among your people, and all your forts will fall, just as at Betharbel, which Shalman[2] destroyed; even mothers and children were dashed to death there. That will also be your fate, you people of Israel, because of your great wickedness. In one morning the king of Israel shall be destroyed.

CHAPTER 11

WHEN ISRAEL WAS A CHILD I loved him as a son and brought him out of Egypt.

2-3 But the more I called to him, the more he rebelled, sacrificing to Baal and burning incense to idols. I trained him from infancy; I taught him to walk; I held him in My arms. But he doesn't know or even care that it was I who raised him.

4-6 As a man would lead his favorite ox,[1] so I led Israel with My ropes of love. I loosened his muzzle so he could eat. I myself have stooped and fed him. But My people shall return to Egypt and Assyria because they won't return to Me. War will swirl through their cities; their enemies will crash through their gates and trap them in their own fortresses.

7-8 My people are determined to desert Me, so I have sentenced them to slavery, and no one shall set them free. Oh, how

*Implied.
[2]Shalman: probably Salaman, King of Moab, who invaded Gilead around 740 B.C.
[1]Judges, chapters 19 and 20.

24

can I give you up, My Ephraim? How can I let you go? How can I forsake you like Admah and Zeboim?[3] My heart cries out within Me; how I long to help you!

9-11 No, I will not punish you as much as My fierce anger tells Me to. This is the last time I will destroy Ephraim. For I am God and not man; I am the Holy One living among you and I did not come to destroy. For the people shall walk after the Lord. I shall roar as a lion (at their enemies)[1] and My people shall return trembling from the west. Like a flock of birds, they will come from Egypt—like doves flying from Assyria. And I will bring them home again; it is a promise from the Lord.

12 Israel surrounds Me with lies and deceit; but Judah still trusts in God and is faithful to the Holy One.

CHAPTER 12

ISRAEL IS CHASING THE WIND, yes, shepherding a whirlwind--a dangerous game![1] For she has given gifts to Egypt and Assyria to get their help, and in return she gets their worthless promises.

2-5 But the Lord is bringing a lawsuit against Judah,[2] too. Judah also will be justly punished for his ways. When he was born, he struggled with his brother; when he became a man, he even fought with God. Yes, he wrestled with the Angel and prevailed. He wept and pleaded for a blessing from Him. He met God there at Bethel face to face. God spoke to him—the Lord, the God of Hosts; Jehovah is His Name.

6 Oh, come back to God. Live by the principles of love and justice, and always be expecting much from Him, your God.

7 But no, My people are like crafty merchants selling from dishonest scales—they love to cheat.

8-9 Ephraim boasts, "I am so rich! I have gotten it all by myself!" But riches can't make up for sin. I am the same Lord, the same God, who delivered you from slavery in Egypt, and I am the One who will consign you to living in tents again, as you do each year at the Tabernacle Feast.

10-11 I sent My prophets to warn you with many a vision and many a parable and dream. But the sins of Gilgal flourish just

[3]Cities of the plain that perished with Sodom and Gomorrah (Deut. 29:23).
[1]Implied.
[2]Literally, "Jacob."

25

the same. Row on row of altars—like furrows in a field—are used for sacrifices to your idols. And Gilead, too, is full of fools[3] who worship idols.

12-14 Jacob fled to Syria and earned a wife by tending sheep. Then the Lord led His people out of Egypt by a prophet, who guided and protected them. But Ephraim has bitterly provoked the Lord. The Lord will sentence him to death as payment for his sins.

CHAPTER 13

IT USED TO BE THAT WHEN ISRAEL SPOKE, the nations shook with fear, for he was a mighty prince; but he worshiped Baal and sealed his doom.

2 And now the people disobey more and more. They melt their silver to mold into idols, formed with skill by the hands of men. "Sacrifice to these!" they say—men kissing calves!

3-5 They shall disappear like morning mist; like dew that quickly dries away; like chaff blown by the wind; like a cloud of smoke. I alone am God, your Lord, and have been ever since I brought you out from Egypt. You have no God but Me, for there is no other Saviour. I took care of you in the wilderness, in that dry and thirsty land.

6-8 But when you had eaten and were satisfied, then you became proud and forgot Me. So I will come upon you like a lion, or a leopard lurking along the road. I will rip you to pieces like a bear whose cubs have been taken away; and like a lion I will devour you.

9-11 O Israel, if I destroy you, who can save you? Where is your king? Why don't you call on him for help? Where are all the leaders of the land? You asked for them, now let them save you! I gave you kings in My anger, and I took them away[1] in My wrath.

12-15 Ephraim's sins are harvested and stored away for punishment. New birth is offered him, but he is like a child resisting in the womb—how stubborn! how foolish! Shall I ransom him from Hell? Shall I redeem him from Death? O Death, bring forth your terrors for his tasting! Oh Grave, demonstrate your plagues! For I will not relent! He was called the most fruitful of all his brothers, but the east wind—a wind of the Lord from the

[3]Or, "vanity."
[1]Probably an allusion to the kings of Israel assassinated during her last tempestuous years: Zechariah, Shallum, Pekahiah.

desert—will blow hard upon him and dry up his land. All his flowing springs and green oases will dry away, and he will die of thirst.

16 Samaria must bear her guilt, for she rebelled against her God. Her people will be killed by the invading army, her babies dashed to death against the ground, her pregnant women ripped open with the sword.

CHAPTER 14

O ISRAEL, RETURN TO THE LORD, YOUR GOD; for you have been crushed by your sins.

2-3 Bring your petition. Come to the Lord and say, "O Lord, take away our sins; be gracious to us and receive us, and we will offer You the sacrifice of praise. Assyria cannot save us, nor can our strength in battle; never again will we call the idols we have made 'our gods'; for in You alone, O Lord, the fatherless find mercy."

4-7 Then I will cure you of idolatry and faithlessness, and My love will know no bounds, for My anger will be forever gone! I will refresh Israel like the dew from heaven; she will blossom as the lily and root deeply in the soil like cedars in Lebanon. Her branches will spread out as beautiful as olive trees, fragrant as the forests of Lebanon. Her people will return from exile far away and rest beneath My shadow. They will be a watered garden and blossom like grapes and be as fragrant as the wines of Lebanon.

8 O Ephraim! Stay away from idols! I am living and strong! I look after you and care for you. I am like an evergreen tree, yielding My fruit to you throughout the year. My mercies never fail.

9 Whoever is wise, let him understand these things. Whoever is intelligent, let him listen. For the paths of the Lord are true and right, and good men walk along them. But sinners trying it will fail.

Maybe they're called Minor Prophets because they aren't very important . . . ?

The Role Of Joel

"LISTEN! WHAT'S THAT NOISE? And what's happened to the sun all of a sudden? It's like night! Grasshoppers? Grasshoppers! Get them out of here! They're down my back! They're crawling up my legs! Oof—I think there's one in my ear!"

A deplorable situation.

But this was not the worst of it. In a short while the grasshopperlike locusts devoured everything green (hurrah, no more broccoli!), and were proceeding to other colors.

Close at their heels came the scorching sun, searing whatever had escaped the hoppers' nearsighted scrutiny.

The land lay like Mother Hubbard's cupboard—empty.

"When do we eat?" was replaced by *"What* do we eat?"

The answer was the same everywhere. "Nothing."

At a time like this, if at no other time, people may turn to God, which gives us some idea of why God portions out such adversity.

The land of Israel was in a mess: the people had forgotten God and His teachings, and everything had gone to pot as a result. To bring them back to Himself, God planned something drastic. The gnawing of the locusts, the pangs of hunger, the shriveling drouth—these *were* drastic. The people were ready to listen as their prophet, Joel, brought them words from God:

"This plague—has such a monstrous thing happened in your days, or even in the days of your fathers? The destruction has been utter. What the cutting locust left, the swarming locust has eaten; what the swarming locust left, the hopping locust has eaten; and what the hopping locust left, the destroying locust has

29

eaten. Your fields are laid waste; the ground mourns; the harvest has perished."

Then Joel told the clergy what to do: "Dress yourselves in sackcloth and plead with God. Declare a fast. Gather the elders and all the inhabitants of the land to the house of the Lord your God, and cry unto Him. He is merciful. Perhaps if you truly repent and return unto Him, He will put an end to this desolation."

The priests put on sackcloth and besought God: "Spare your people, O Lord. Don't let the heathen nations be able to laugh and say, 'Where is this God they say they believe in? Can't He help them?'"

When the Lord saw that they were truly repentant, He had pity on them and told Joel to tell the people, "Behold, I will send to you grain, wine, and oil, and you shall eat in plenty and be satisfied, and praise the name of the Lord your God, who has dealt wondrously with you. And you shall know that I, the Lord, am your God, and there is none else."

Then God used this occasion—the infestation of grasshoppers—not only to bring the people back to a living relationship with Himself, but also to prepare them for Judgment Day:

"I will give forewarning in the heavens and on the earth—blood and fire and columns of smoke. The sun shall be turned to darkness, and the moon to blood before the great and terrible Day of the Lord comes. And it shall come to pass that all who call upon the name of the Lord shall be saved.

"For behold, in those days I will gather all the nations and bring them down to the valley of Jehoshaphat, and I will enter into judgment with them there."

But God promised that before that day He would send His Holy Spirit:

"And it shall come to pass, that I will pour out my Spirit on all flesh; your sons and your daughters shall prophesy, your old men shall dream dreams, and your young men shall see visions."

And so God, through Joel, had brought His people once more back to Himself.

As for the locusts, God shunted them off into the desert of Arabia, from which, in due time, a stench wafted clear back to Israel. But the stench was perfume to the olfactory nerves of the delivered Israelites. The grasshopper scourge was over. The people were once more ready to serve God with their whole hearts.

Joel

CHAPTER 1

THIS MESSAGE CAME FROM THE LORD TO JOEL, *son of Pethuel:*

2-4 Listen, you aged men of Israel! Everyone, listen! In all your lifetime, yes, in all your history, have you ever heard of such a thing as I am going to tell you? In years to come, tell your children about it; pass the awful story down from generation to generation: For after the cutter-locusts finish eating your crops, the swarmer-locusts will take what's left! After them will come the hopper-locusts! And then the stripper-locusts, too!

5-7 Wake up and weep, you drunkards; for all the grapes are ruined and all your wine is gone! A vast army of locusts[1] covers the land. It is a terrible army too numerous to count, with teeth as sharp as those of lions! They have ruined My vines and stripped the bark from the fig trees, leaving trunks and branches white and bare.

8-10 Weep with sorrow, as a virgin weeps whose fiancé is dead. Gone are the offerings of grain and wine to bring to the temple of the Lord; the priests are starving. Hear the crying of these ministers of God. The fields are bare of crops. Sorrow and sadness are everywhere. The grain, the grapes, the olive oil are gone.

11-12 Well may you farmers stand so shocked and stricken; well may you vinedressers weep. Weep for the wheat and the barley too, for they are gone. The grapevines are dead; the fig trees are dying; the pomegranates wither; the apples shrivel on the trees; all joy has withered with them.

13-17 O priests, robe yourselves in sackcloth. O ministers of my God, lie all night before the altar, weeping. For there are no more offerings of grain and wine for you. Announce a fast; call a solemn meeting. Gather the elders and all the people into the Temple of the Lord your God, and weep before Him there. Alas, this terrible day of punishment[2] is on the way. Destruction

[1]Literally, "a nation."
[2]Or, "the Day of the Lord."

from the Almighty is almost here! Our food will disappear before our eyes; all joy and gladness will be ended in the Temple of our God. The seed rots in the ground; the barns and granaries are empty; the grain has dried up in the fields.

18-20 The cattle groan with hunger; the herds stand perplexed for there is no pasture for them; the sheep bleat in misery. Lord, help us! For the heat has withered the pastures and burned up all the trees. Even the wild animals cry to You for help, for there is no water for them. The creeks are dry and the pastures are scorched.

CHAPTER 2

SOUND THE ALARM IN JERUSALEM! Let the blast of the warning trumpet be heard upon My holy mountain! Let everyone tremble in fear, for the day of the Lord's judgment approaches.

2-3 It is a day of darkness and gloom, of black clouds and thick darkness. What a mighty army! It covers the mountains like night! How great, how powerful these "people" are! The likes of them have not been seen before, and never will again throughout the generations of the world! Fire goes before them and follows them on every side! Ahead of them the land lies fair as Eden's Garden in all its beauty, but they destroy it to the ground; not one thing escapes.

4-10 They look like tiny horses, and they run as fast. Look at them leaping along the tops of the mountain! Listen to the noise they make, like the rumbling of chariots, or the roar of fire sweeping across a field; and like a mighty army moving into battle. Fear grips the waiting people; their faces grow pale with fright. These "soldiers" charge like infantry; they scale the walls like picked and trained commandos. Straight forward they march, never breaking ranks. They never crowd each other. Each is right in place. No weapon can stop them. They swarm upon the city; they run up on the walls; they climb up into the houses, coming like thieves through the windows. The earth quakes before them and the heavens tremble. The sun and moon are obscured and the stars are hid

11 The Lord leads them with a shout. This is His mighty army and they follow His orders. The day of the judgment of the Lord is an awesome, terrible thing. Who can endure it?

12-14   That is why the Lord says, "Turn to Me now, while there is time. Give Me all your hearts. Come with fasting, weeping, mourning. Let your remorse tear your hearts and not your garments." Return to the Lord your God, for He is gracious and merciful. He is not easily angered; He is full of kindness, and anxious not to punish you. Who knows? Perhaps even yet He will decide to let you alone and give you a blessing instead of His terrible curse. Perhaps He will give you so much that you can offer your grain and wine to the Lord as before!

15-17   Sound the trumpet in Zion! Call a fast and gather all the people together for a solemn meeting. Bring everyone—the elders, the children, and even the babies. Call the bridegroom from his quarters and the bride from her privacy. The priests, the ministers of God, will stand between the people and the altar, weeping; and they will pray, "Spare Your people, O our God; don't let the heathen rule them, for they belong to You. Don't let them be disgraced by the taunts of the heathen who say, 'Where is this God of theirs? How weak and helpless He must be!'"

18-19   Then the Lord will pity His people and be indignant for the honor of His land! He will reply, "See, I am sending you much corn and wine and oil, to fully satisfy your need. No longer will I make you a laughingstock among the nations.

20   "I will remove these armies from the north and send them far away; I will turn them back into the parched wastelands where they will die; half shall be driven into the Dead Sea and the rest into the Mediterranean, and then their rotting stench will rise upon the land. The Lord has done a mighty miracle for you.

21-22   "Fear not, My people; be glad now and rejoice, for He has done amazing things for you. Let the flocks and herds forget their hunger: the pastures will turn green again. The trees will bear their fruit: the fig trees and grapevines will flourish once more.

23-27   "Rejoice, O people of Jerusalem, rejoice in the Lord your God! For the rains He sends are tokens of forgiveness. Once more the autumn rains will come, as well as those of spring. The threshing floors will pile high again with wheat, and the presses overflow with olive oil and wine. And I will give you back the crops the locusts ate!—My great destroying army that I sent against you. Once again you will have all the food you want. Praise the Lord, who does these miracles for you. And never again will My people experience disaster such as this. And you will know that I am here among My people Israel, and that I alone am the Lord, your God. And My people shall never again be dealt a blow like this.

28-30 "After I have poured out My rains again, I will pour out My Spirit upon all of you! Your sons and daughters will prophesy; your old men will dream dreams, and your young men see visions. And I will pour out My Spirit even on your slaves, men and women alike, and put strange symbols in the earth and sky—blood and fire and pillars of smoke.

31-32 "The sun will be turned into darkness and the moon to blood before the great and terrible Day of the Lord shall come. Everyone who calls upon the name of the Lord will be saved; even in Jerusalem some will escape, just as the Lord has promised; for He has chosen some to survive."

CHAPTER 3

AT THAT TIME, when I restore the prosperity of Judah and Jerusalem," says the Lord,

2-3 "I will gather the armies of the world into the Valley Where Jehovah Judges[1] and punish them there for harming My people, for scattering My inheritance among the nations and dividing up My land. They divided up My people as their slaves; they traded a young lad for a prostitute, and a little girl for wine enough to get drunk.

4-8 "Tyre and Sidon, don't you try to interfere! Are you trying to take revenge on Me, you cities of Philistia? Beware, for I will strike back swiftly, and return the harm to your own heads. You have taken My silver and gold and all My precious treasures and carried them off to your heathen temples. You have sold the people of Judah and Jerusalem to the Greeks, who took them far from their own land. But I will bring them back again from all these places you have sold them to, and I will pay you back for all that you have done. I will sell your sons and daughters to the people of Judah and they will sell them to the Sabeans far away. This is a promise from the Lord."

9-11 Announce this far and wide: Get ready for war! Conscript your best soldiers; collect all your armies. Melt your plowshares into swords and beat your pruning hooks into spears. Let

[1]Or, "Valley of Jehoshaphat."

34

the weak be strong. Gather together and come, all nations everywhere. And now, O Lord, bring down Your warriors!

12-13 Collect the nations; bring them to the Valley of Jehoshaphat; for there I will sit to pronounce judgment on them all. Now let the sickle do its work; the harvest is ripe and waiting. Tread the winepress, for it is full to overflowing with the wickedness of these men.

14 Multitudes, multitudes waiting in the valley for the verdict of their doom! For the Day of the Lord is near, in the Valley of Judgment.

15-19 The sun and moon will be darkened and the stars withdraw their light. The Lord shouts from His temple in Jerusalem and the earth and sky began to shake. But to His people Israel, the Lord will be very gentle. He is their Refuge and Strength. "Then you shall know at last that I am the Lord your God in Zion, My holy mountain. Jerusalem shall be Mine forever; the time will come when no foreign armies will pass through her any more. Sweet wine will drip from the mountains, and the hills shall flow with milk. Water will fill the dry stream beds of Judah, and a fountain will burst forth from the temple of the Lord to water Acacia Valley. Egypt will be destroyed and Edom too, because of their violence against the Jews, for they killed innocent people in those nations.

20-21 "But Israel will prosper forever, and Jerusalem will thrive as generations pass. For I will avenge the blood of My people; I will not clear their oppressors of guilt. For My home is in Jerusalem² with My people."

²Literally, "Zion."

*The printer could leave the
Minor Prophets out of the Bible and most
people wouldn't know the difference.*

Why Amos Is Famous

IT WAS AN UNUSUAL ASSIGNMENT: *High-tail it to the neighboring country and warn the people that they're bringing down disaster upon themselves.*

But Amos packed and went.

Upon reaching Bethel, he climbed up on whatever was used for a soapbox in those days and began:

"You have become rich and have forgotten many things. Look at you! You hate to see the Sabbath come because you're so greedy to earn more money that you can't even take time out to go to worship! You cheat your customers by loading the bottoms of the grain sacks with stones! You water down the milk! You give the scales a sly assist with your thumb when you weigh purchases! You sell the poor into slavery the moment they can't pay their bills! You care not one iota for those who suffer! You sell the penniless for a pair of shoes!

"You are well-to-do and proud of it, but in your soul is famine.

"You began as God's chosen ones; now all that is forgotten. Now you waste your lives in chasing pleasure, in piling up even more wealth, in stomping on the poor—all the time drifting further from the God who made you.

"You are no better than cattle!

"Mark my words: there is no end to all this but decay and death!"

At this point at least one of the listeners had heard enough. Ready to blow a fuse, Amaziah, the local priest, dispatched a messenger. "Go tell the king that Amos is conspiring against him!" he raged. "Tell him," he went on, repeating the words that Amos was now saying, "that Amos predicts that he, the king, is going to be killed by a sword, that Israel will be conquered, and that all the people will be led away as slaves!"

Without waiting to see the courier off, Amaziah rammed his way through the crowd. How dare this young upstart Amos come into his parish and carry on so!

He stormed up to the front and grabbed Amos by the shoulder of his shepherd's garb. "All right," he growled, "get moving! We don't need your half-baked ideas around here. Go back to where you came from and prophesy there. Maybe they have a little more stomach for your words than we do!"

Amos did not budge. He just went on giving his message: "I was neither a prophet nor the son of a prophet, but a sheep-herder and keeper of a fig orchard until the day God called me and said, 'Go, prophesy to My people Israel.' God has sent me here to tell you these things, and I'm not through yet. Therefore, hear the words of the Lord!"

Turning again to his audience, Amos put the finishing touches on his sermon.

"You have forgotten God. Behold, He will send a famine upon your land; not a famine of bread, but a famine of hearing the words of the Lord. You shall wander from sea to sea and from north to south to seek the word of the Lord, and you shall not find it.

"Behold, the eyes of the Lord God are upon this sinful kingdom, and He will destroy it off the face of the earth, saving only the house of Jacob."

And, having completed his message, Amos climbed down off his soapbox and went back to Tekoa to tend his flocks, thus ending one of the shortest preaching campaigns on record.

How effective was his speech?

Seemingly no one paid too much attention to what he said. Israel, carrying on in its same blind way, was overcome by an invader and led away into captivity—just as Amos had foretold. But during their days in slavery the people began to remember Amos' words, repented, were restored to God, and, ultimately, to their homeland.

And Amos, the quiet, rural servant of God, lived out his days peacefully among his sheep and sycamore trees, writing the book that we carry around in our Bibles today. Amos had started a fire in the hearts of God's people that was never to go out.

Amos

CHAPTER 1

AMOS WAS A HERDSMAN living in the village of Tekoa. All day long he sat on the hillsides watching the sheep, keeping them from straying.

2 One day, in a vision, God told him some of the things that were going to happen to his nation, Israel. This vision came to him at the time Uzziah was king of Judah, and while Jeroboam (son of Joash) was king of Israel—two years before the earthquake. This is his report of what he saw and heard: The Lord roared—like a ferocious lion from his lair—from His temple on Mount Zion. And suddenly the lush pastures of Mount Carmel withered and dried, and all the shepherds mourned.

3-5 The Lord says, "The people of Damascus have sinned again and again, and I will not forget it. I will not leave her unpunished any more. For they have threshed My people in Gilead like grain is threshed with iron rods. So I will set fire to King Hazael's palace, destroying the strong fortress of Benhadad. I will snap the bars that locked the gates of Damascus, and kill her people as far away as the plain of Aven; and the people of Syria shall return to Kir[1] as slaves." The Lord has spoken.

6-8 The Lord says, "Gaza has sinned again and again, and I will not forget it. I will not leave her unpunished any more. For she sent My people into exile, selling them as slaves in Edom. So I will set fire to the walls of Gaza, and all her forts shall be destroyed. I will kill the people of Ashdod, and destroy Ekron and the king of Ashkelon; all Philistines left will perish." The Lord has spoken.

9-10 The Lord says, "The people of Tyre have sinned again and again, and I will not forget it. I will not leave them unpunished any more. For they broke their treaty with their brother, Israel; they attacked and conquered him, and led him into slavery to Edom. So I will set fire to the walls of Tyre, and it will burn down all his forts and palaces."

[1]Decreeing that the Syrians should go back to Kir as slaves was like saying to the Israelites that they must go back to Egypt as slaves, for the Syrians had made their exodus from Kir and now were free (See 9:7).

11-12   The Lord says, "Edom has sinned again and again, and I will not forget it. I will not leave him unpunished any more. For he chased his brother, Israel, with the sword; he was pitiless in unrelenting anger. So I will set fire to Teman, and it will burn down all the forts of Bozrah."[2]

13-15   The Lord says, "The people of Ammon have sinned again and again, and I will not forget it. I will not leave them unpunished any more. For in their wars in Gilead to enlarge their borders, they committed cruel crimes, ripping open pregnant women with their swords. So I will set fire to the walls of Rabah, and it will burn down their forts and palaces; there will be wild shouts of battle like a whirlwind in a mighty storm. And their king and his princes will go into exile together." The Lord has spoken.

CHAPTER 2

THE LORD SAYS, "The people of Moab have sinned again and again, and I will not forget it. I will not leave them unpunished any more. For they desecrated the tombs of the kings of Edom, with no respect for the dead.

2-3   Now in return I will send fire upon Moab, and it will destroy all the palaces in Kirioth. Moab shall go down in tumult as the warriors shout and trumpets blare. And I will destroy their king and slay all the leaders under him." The Lord has spoken.

4-5   The Lord says, "The people of Judah have sinned again and again, and I will not forget it. I will not leave them unpunished any more. For they have rejected the laws of God, refusing to obey Him. They have hardened their hearts and sinned as their fathers did. So I will destroy Judah with fire, and burn down all Jerusalem's palaces and forts."

6-8   The Lord says, "The people of Israel have sinned again and again, and I will not forget it. I will not leave them unpunished any more. For they have perverted justice by accepting bribes, and sold into slavery the poor who can't repay their debts; they trade them for a pair of shoes. They trample the poor in the dust and kick aside the meek. And a man and his father defile the same temple-girl, corrupting My holy name. At their religious feasts they lounge in clothing stolen from their

[2]Teman was in the north of Edom, and Bozrah in the south. The entire country would be devastated.

40

debtors,[1] and in My own Temple they offer sacrifices of wine they purchased with stolen money.

9-12 "Yet think of all I did for them! I cleared the land of the Amorites before them—the Amorites, as tall as cedar trees, and strong as oaks! But I lopped off their fruit and cut their roots. And I brought you out from Egypt and led you through the desert forty years, to possess the land of the Amorites. And I chose your sons to be Nazirites[2] and prophets—can you deny this, Israel?" asks the Lord. "But you caused the Nazirites to sin by urging them to drink your wine, and you silenced My prophets, telling them, 'Shut up!'

13 "Therefore I will make you groan as a wagon groans that is loaded down with sheaves.

14-16 "Your swiftest warriors will stumble in flight. The strong will all be weak, and the great ones can no longer save themselves. The archer's aim will fail, the swiftest runners won't be fast enough to flee, and even the best of horsemen can't outrun the danger then. The most courageous of your mighty men will drop their weapons and run for their lives that day." The Lord God has spoken.

CHAPTER 3

LISTEN! THIS IS YOUR DOOM! It is spoken by the Lord against both Israel and Judah—against the entire family I brought from Egypt:

2 "Of all the peoples of the earth, I have chosen you alone. That is why I must punish you the more for all your sins.

3 For how can we walk together with your sins between us?

4-6 Would I be roaring as a lion unless I had a reason? The fact is, I am getting ready to destroy you. Even a young lion, when it growls, shows it is ready for its food. A trap doesn't snap shut unless it is stepped on; your punishment is well-deserved. The alarm has sounded—listen and fear! For I, the Lord, am sending disaster into your land.

7 But always, first of all, I warn you through My prophets. This I now have done."

8 The Lion has roared—tremble in fear. The Lord God has sounded your doom—I dare not refuse to proclaim it.

[1] Under Mosaic Law, it was illegal to keep pledged clothing of debtors overnight. See Exodus 22:26.
[2] See Numbers, chapter 6.

9-11 Call together the Assyrian and Egyptian leaders, saying, "Take your seats now on the mountains of Samaria to witness the scandalous spectacle of all Israel's crimes. My people have forgotten what it means to do right," says the Lord. "Their beautiful homes are full of the loot from their thefts and banditry. Therefore," the Lord God says, "an enemy is coming! He is surrounding them and will shatter their forts and plunder those beautiful homes."

12-15 The Lord says, "A shepherd tried to rescue his sheep from a lion, but it was too late: he snatched from the lion's mouth two legs and a piece of ear. So it will be when the Israelites in Samaria are finally rescued—all they will have left is half a chair and a tattered pillow." Listen to this announcement, and publish it throughout all Israel, says the Lord, the God of Hosts: "On the same day that I punish Israel for her sins, I will also destroy the idol altars at Bethel. The horns of the altar will be cut off and fall to the ground. And I will destroy the beautiful homes of the wealthy—their winter mansions and their summer houses, too—and demolish their ivory palaces."

CHAPTER 4

LISTEN TO ME, you "fat cows" of Bashan living in Samaria —you women who encourage your husbands to rob the poor and crush the needy—you who never have enough to drink!

2-3 The Lord God has sworn by His holiness that the time will come when He will put hooks in your noses and lead you away like the cattle you are; they will drag the last of you away with fishhooks! You will be hauled from your beautiful homes and tossed out through the nearest breach in the wall. The Lord has said it.

4-5 Go ahead and sacrifice to idols at Bethel and Gilgal. Keep disobeying—your sins are mounting up. Sacrifice each morning and bring your tithes twice a week! Go through all your proper forms and give extra offerings. How you pride yourselves and crow about it everywhere!

6-8 "I sent you hunger," says the Lord, "but it did no good; you still would not return to Me. I ruined your crops by holding back the rain three months before the harvest. I sent rain on one city, but not another. While rain fell on one field, another was dry and withered. People from two or three cities would make their weary journey for a drink of water to a city that had rain, but there wasn't ever enough. Yet you wouldn't return to Me," says the Lord.

9 "I sent blight and mildew on your farms and your vineyards; the locusts ate your figs and olive trees. And still you wouldn't return to Me," says the Lord.

10 "I sent you plagues like those of Egypt long ago. I killed your lads in war and drove away your horses. The stench of death was terrible to smell. And yet you refused to come.

11 "I destroyed some of your cities, as I did Sodom and Gomorrah; those left are like half-burned firebrands snatched away from fire. And still you won't return to Me," says the Lord. "Therefore I will bring upon you all these further evils I have spoken of.

12-13 "Prepare to meet your God in judgment, Israel. For you are dealing with the One who formed the mountains and made the winds, and knows your every thought; He turns the morning to darkness and crushes down the mountains underneath His feet: Jehovah, the Lord, the God of Hosts, is His name."

CHAPTER 5

SADLY I SING this song of grief for you, O Israel:

2 "Beautiful Israel lies broken and crushed upon the ground and cannot rise. No one will help her. She is left alone to die."

3-5 For the Lord God says, "The city that sends a thousand men to battle, a hundred will return. The city that sends a hundred, only ten will come back alive." The Lord says to the people of Israel, "Seek Me—and live. Don't seek the idols of Bethel, Gilgal, or Beersheba; for the people of Gilgal will be carried off to exile, and those of Bethel shall surely come to grief."

6-7 Seek the Lord and live, or else He will sweep like fire through Israel and consume her, and none of the idols in Bethel can put it out. O evil men, you make "justice" a bitter pill for the poor and oppressed. "Righteousness" and "fair play" are meaningless fictions to you!

8 Seek Him who created the Seven Stars and the constellation Orion; who turns darkness into morning, and day into night; who calls forth the water from the ocean and pours it out as rain upon the land. The Lord, Jehovah, is His name.

43

9 With blinding speed and violence He brings destruction on the strong, breaking all defenses.

10-13 How you hate honest judges! How you despise people who tell the truth! You trample the poor and steal their smallest crumb by all your taxes, fines, and usury; therefore you will never live in the beautiful stone houses you are building, nor drink the wine from the lush vineyards you are planting. For many and great are your sins. I know them all so well. You are the enemies of everything good; you take bribes; you refuse justice to the poor. Therefore those who are wise will not try to interfere with the Lord in the dread Day of your punishment.

14-16 Be good, flee evil—and live! Then the Lord God of Hosts will truly be your Helper, as you have claimed He is. Hate evil and love the good; remodel your courts into true halls of justice. Perhaps even yet the Lord God of Hosts will have mercy on His people who remain. Therefore the Lord God of Hosts says this: "There will be crying in all the streets and every road. Call for the farmers to weep with you, too; call for professional mourners to wail and lament.

17-19 "There will be sorrow and crying in every vineyard. For I will pass through and destroy. You say, 'If only the Day of the Lord were here, for then God would deliver us from all our foes.' But you have no idea what you ask. For that Day will *not* be light and prosperity, but darkness and doom! How terrible the darkness will be for you; not a ray of joy or hope will shine. In that Day you will be as a man who is chased by a lion—and met by a bear; or a man in a dark room who leans against a wall—and puts his hand on a snake.

20-27 "Yes, that will be a dark and hopeless day for you. I hate your show and pretence—your hypocrisy of 'honoring' Me with your religious feasts and solemn assemblies. I will not accept your burnt-offerings and thank-offerings. I will not look at your offerings of peace. Away with your hymns of praise—they are mere noise to My ears. I will not listen to your music, no matter how lovely it is. I want to see a mighty flood of justice—a torrent of doing good. You sacrificed to Me for forty years while you were in the desert, Israel—but always your real interest has been in your heathen gods—in Sakkuth your king, and in Kaiwan, your god of the stars, and in all the images of them you made. So I will send them into captivity with you far to the east of Damascus," says the Lord, the God of Hosts.

CHAPTER 6

WOE TO THOSE LOUNGING IN LUXURY at Jerusalem
and Samaria, so famous and popular among the people of Israel.

2-3 Go over to Calneh and see what happened there; then go
to great Hamath and down to Gath in the Philistines' land. Once
these cities were better and greater than you, but look at them
now. You push away all thought of punishment awaiting you,
but by your deeds you bring the Day of Judgment near.

4-9 You lie on ivory beds surrounded with luxury, eating the
meat of the tenderest lambs and the choicest calves. You sing idle
songs to the sound of the harp, and fancy yourselves to be as
great musicians as King David was. You drink wine by the
bucketful and perfume yourselves with sweet ointments, caring
nothing at all that your brothers need your help. Therefore you
will be the first to be taken as slaves; suddenly your revelry will
end. Jehovah, the Lord God of Hosts, has sworn by His own
Name, "I despise the pride and false glory of Israel, and hate
their beautiful homes. I will turn over this city and everything in
it to her enemies." If there are as few as ten of them left, and
even one house, they too will perish.

10-11 A man's uncle will be the only one left to bury him,
and when he goes in to carry his body from the house, he will ask
the only one still alive inside, "Are any others left?" And the
answer will be, "No," and he will add, "Shhh . . . don't mention
the Name of the Lord—He might hear you." For the Lord
commanded this: That homes both great and small should be
smashed to pieces.

12 Can horses run on rocks? Can oxen plow the sea? Stupid
even to ask, but no more stupid than what you do when you
make a mockery of justice, and corrupt and sour all that should
be good and right.

13 And just as stupid is your rejoicing in how great you are,
when you are less than nothing! And priding yourselves on your
own tiny power!

14 "O Israel, I will bring against you a nation that will
bitterly oppress you from your northern boundary to your southern tip, all the way from Hamath to the brook of Arabah," says
the Lord, the God of Hosts.

THIS IS WHAT the Lord God showed me in a vision: He was preparing a vast swarm of locusts to destroy all the main crop that sprang up after the first mowing, which went as taxes to the king.

2-3 They ate everything in sight. Then I said, "O Lord God, please forgive Your people! Don't send them this plague! If You turn against Israel, what hope is there? For Israel is so small!" So the Lord relented, and did not fulfill the vision. "I won't do it," He told me.

4-6 Then the Lord God showed me a great fire He had prepared to punish them; it had burned up the waters and was devouring the entire land. Then I said, "O Lord God, please don't do it. If you turn against them, what hope is there? For Israel is so small!" Then the Lord turned from this plan too, and said, "I won't do that either."

7-9 Then He showed me this: the Lord was standing beside a wall built with a plumbline, checking it with a plumbline to see if it was straight. And the Lord said to me, "Amos, what do you see?"

I answered, "A plumbline."

And He replied, "I will test My people with a plumbline. I will no longer turn away from punishing. The idol altars and temples of Israel will be destroyed; and I will destroy the dynasty of King Jeroboam by the sword."

10-11 But when Amaziah, the priest of Bethel, heard what Amos was saying, he rushed a message to Jeroboam, the king: "Amos is a traitor to our nation and is plotting your death. This is intolerable. It will lead to rebellion all across the land. He says you will be killed, and Israel will be sent far away into exile and slavery."

12-13 Then Amaziah sent orders to Amos, "Get out of here, you prophet, you! Flee to the land of Judah and do your prophesying there! Don't bother us here with your visions; not here in the capital, where the king's chapel is!"

14-17 But Amos replied, "I am not really one of the prophets. I do not come from a family of prophets. I am just a herdsman and fruit picker. But the Lord took me from caring for the flocks and told me, 'Go and prophesy to My people Israel.' Now therefore listen to this message to you from the Lord. You say, 'Don't prophesy against Israel.' The Lord's reply is this: 'Because of your interference, your wife will become a prostitute in this city, and your sons and daughters will be killed and your land divided up. You yourself will die in a heathen land, and the people of Israel will certainly become slaves in exile, far from their land.' "

CHAPTER 8

THEN THE LORD GOD SHOWED ME, in a vision, a basket full of ripe fruit.

2 "What do you see, Amos?" He asked. I replied, "A basket full of ripe fruit." Then the Lord said, "This fruit represents My people Israel—ripe for punishment. I will not defer their punishment again.

3 The riotous sound of singing in the temple will turn to weeping then. Dead bodies will be scattered everywhere. They will be carried out of the city in silence." The Lord has spoken.

4-10 Listen, you merchants who rob the poor, trampling on the needy; you who long for the Sabbath to end and the religious holidays to be over, so you can get out and start cheating again—using your weighted scales and under-sized measures; you who make slaves of the poor, buying them for their debt of a piece of silver or a pair of shoes, or selling them your moldy wheat—the Lord, the Pride of Israel, has sworn: "I won't forget your deeds! The land will tremble as it awaits its doom, and everyone will mourn. It will rise up like the River Nile at floodtime, toss about, and sink again. At that time I will make the sun go down at noon and darken the earth in the daytime. And I will turn your parties into times of mourning, and your songs of joy will be turned into cries of despair. You will wear funeral clothes and shave your heads as signs of sorrow, as if your only son had died; bitter, bitter will be that Day.

11-12 "The time is surely coming," says the Lord God, "when I will send a famine on the land—not a famine of bread or water, but of hearing the words of the Lord. Men will wander everywhere from sea to sea, seeking the Word of the Lord, searching, running here and going there, but will not find it.

13-14 "Beautiful girls and fine young men alike will grow faint and weary, thirsting for the Word of God. And those who worship the idols of Samaria, Dan, and Beersheba shall fall and never rise again."

I SAW THE LORD standing beside the altar saying, "Smash the tops of the pillars and shake the temple until the pillars crumble and the roof crashes down upon the people below. Though they run, they will not escape; they all will be killed.

2-4 "Though they dig down to Sheol, I will reach down and pull them up; though they climb into the heavens, I will bring them down. Though they hide among the rocks at the top of Carmel, I will search them out and capture them. Though they hide at the bottom of the ocean, I will send the sea-serpent after them to bite and destroy them. Though they volunteer for exile, I will command the sword to kill them there. I will see to it that they receive evil and not good."

5-6 The Lord God of Hosts touches the land and it melts; and all its people mourn. It rises like the River Nile in Egypt, and then sinks again. The upper stories of His home are in the heavens, the first floor on the earth. He calls for the vapor to rise from the ocean and pours it down as rain upon the ground. Jehovah, the Lord, is His Name.

7-10 "O people of Israel, are you any more to Me than the Ethiopians are? Have not I, who brought you out of Egypt, done as much for other people, too? I brought the Philistines from Caphtor and the Syrians out of Kir. The eyes of the Lord God are watching Israel, that sinful nation, and I will root her up and scatter her across the world. Yet I have promised that this rooting out will not be permanent. For I have commanded that Israel be sifted by the other nations as grain is sifted in a sieve, yet not one true kernel will be lost. But all these sinners who say, 'God will not touch us,' will die by the sword.

11-14 "Then, at that time, I will rebuild the City of David, which is now lying in ruins, and return it to its former glory, and Israel will possess what is left of Edom, and of all the nations that belong to Me." For so the Lord, who plans it all, has said. "The time will come when there will be such abundance of crops, that the harvest time will scarcely end before the farmer starts again to sow another crop, and the terraces of grapes upon the hills of Israel will drip sweet wine! I will restore the fortunes of My people Israel, and they shall rebuild their ruined cities, and live in them again; and they shall plant vineyards and gardens and eat their crops and drink their wine.

15 "I will firmly plant them there upon the land that I have given them; they shall not be pulled up again," says the Lord your God.

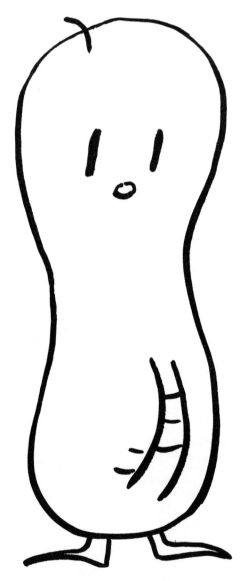

Read the Minor Prophets!
Do you think I'm some kind of a nut?

An Unmighty Fortress

BANG! GRIND! CLASH!

High in the jagged mountains of Edom a determined band of men, up before dawn, hurriedly lashed on their swords and shields. A last look at their city, strategically set among the rugged cliffs, then on to battle.

After an unusually bloody conflict, the city of Jerusalem was theirs, and they dashed from house to house, seizing whatever caught their eye.

Then, towering over their pleading victims, they burst into derisive laughter.

Laughter?

Had they forgotten that they and the Israelites were brothers? How could these descendants of Esau deal so treacherously with the descendants of his twin, Jacob?

Nor was this their first raid. On several other infamous occasions, the fighting men of Edom had swept down out of their mountain fortress south of the Dead Sea in what is today the kingdom of Jordan and plundered the Israelites.

Was there to be no end to this family feud?

Certainly it was a sad historical fact that Esau had given over his birthright to Jacob for the ancient equivalent of stew, and that Jacob had later tricked his father Isaac into also giving him the family blessing. Old Isaac, blind as he was, could hardly be blamed—with goatskin tied securely in place, Jacob's neck and arms *felt* like Esau's hairy ones.

In those days a birthright was nothing to be sniffed at. It gave the firstborn the right not only to inherit a double share of his father's property; it also passed on to him the leadership of the family or clan.

51

In the case of Jacob and Esau, the birthright meant something additional, something of even greater value. It meant the privilege of being in the line of the ancestors of Christ, for God had promised Abraham that through him, and his son Isaac, and Isaac's son, the very Son of God would someday descend.

All this apparently failed to impress Esau. If he had thought enough of his birthright, he would not have traded it off so carelessly to his brother.

And now Esau's descendants, the Edomites, were drifting along in the same spiritually careless way. They no longer were even Jews. For all practical purposes, they had no religion. Business had become their reigning god; the buying and selling of sheep and cattle had become their sole form of worship; and perhaps the only prayer that fell from their lips was, "Hail, Money, successor to God."

The Edomites had a long history of malice toward Israel. Back when Moses was leading the Children of Israel out of Egypt into the Promised Land, he asked permission from the Edomites to pass through their land, which would have cut the length of the journey considerably.

When the men of Edom came charging out to meet them in full battle armor, Moses got his answer, and took the long way around.

God was not drowsing during all this. He gave His prophet Obadiah these words to deliver to Edom: "You who live in the clefts of the rock, you who say, 'No one will ever be able to bring us down from our impenetrable city'—to you I say, 'I will bring you down.' Behold, I will make you utterly despised among the nations."

God vowed to mete out to them the consequences of their cruelty. "Because of the violence you have done to your brother Jacob, you will live hereafter in shame, and in time I will sweep every man of you from off the face of the earth. There shall be no survivor of the house of Esau.

"As you have done, so shall it be done to you. Your deeds shall return upon your own head."

We do not know when, or where, or how Obadiah delivered this prophecy that is recorded in the shortest book of the Old Testament (one chapter, 21 verses), but history shows that the prophecy was fulfilled—and speedily. Just a few years later Edom was attacked and practically annihilated.

From the few survivors later came the unsavory King Herods—no more saintly nor esteemed among the Israelites than the earlier Edomites.

In due time, there remained not a single branch or twig upon the family tree of Edom. The men from the *un*mighty mountainside fortress were no more, just as Obadiah had prophesied.

Obadiah had just one more prophecy to make, one that stands today: "The Lord shall be King!"

Obadiah

IN A VISION, the Lord God showed Obadiah the future of the land of Edom.[1]

"A report has come from the Lord," he said, "that God has sent an ambassador to the nations with this message: 'Attention! You are to send your armies against Edom and destroy her!'"

* * * *

2-4 I will cut you down to size among the nations, Edom, making you small and despised. You are proud because you live in those high, inaccessible cliffs. "Who can ever reach us way up here!" you boast. Don't fool yourselves! Though you soar as high as eagles, and build your nest among the stars, I will bring you plummeting down, says the Lord.

5-9 Far better it would be for you if thieves had come at night to plunder you—for they would not take everything! or if your vineyards were robbed of all their fruit—for at least the gleanings would be left! Every nook and cranny will be searched and robbed, and every treasure found and taken. All your allies will turn against you and help to push you out of your land. They will promise peace while plotting your destruction. Your trusted friends will set traps for you and all your counter-strategy will fail. In that day not one wise man[2] will be left in all of Edom! says the Lord. For I will fill the wise men of Edom with stupidity. The mightiest soldiers of Teman will be confused, and helpless to prevent the slaughter.

10-11 And why? Because of what you did to your brother Israel. Now your sins will be exposed for all to see; ashamed and defenseless, you will be cut off forever. For you deserted Israel in his time of need. You stood aloof, refusing to lift a finger to help him when invaders carried off his wealth and divided Jerusalem among them by lot; you were as one of his enemies.

12-15 You should not have done it. You should not have gloated when they took him far away to foreign lands; you

[1] A nation southeast of Israel, including Petra, the city hewn from rocks; her southern boundary was on the Gulf of Aqaba.
[2] Edom was noted for her wise men; Eliphaz, the wisest of Job's three friends, was from Teman, 5 miles east of Petra, in Edom.

should not have rejoiced in the day of his misfortune; you should not have mocked in his time of need. You yourselves went into the land of Israel in the day of his calamity and looted him. You made yourselves rich at his expense. You stood at the crossroads and killed those trying to escape; you captured the survivors and returned them to their enemies in that terrible time of his distress. The Lord's vengeance will soon fall upon all heathen nations. As you have done to Israel, so will it be done to you. Your acts will boomerang upon your heads.

16-19 You drank My cup of punishment upon My holy mountain, and the nations round about will drink it, too; yes, drink and stagger back and disappear from history, no longer nations any more. But Jerusalem will become a refuge, a way of escape. Israel will reoccupy the land. Israel will be a fire that sets the dry fields of Edom aflame. There will be no survivors, for the Lord has spoken. Then My people who live in the Negeb shall occupy the hill country of Edom; those living in Judean lowlands shall possess the Philistine plains, and repossess the fields of Ephraim and Samaria. And the people of Benjamin shall possess Gilead.

20 The Israeli exiles shall return and occupy the Phoenician coastal strip as far north as Zarephath. Those exiled in Asia Minor shall return to their homeland and conquer the Negeb's outlying villages.

21 For deliverers will come to Jerusalem and rule all Edom. And the Lord shall be King!

*I don't think the Minor Prophets
worked in mines, but there's something
about them I dig . . .*

The Fish That Went Manning

THERE HE WAS, a slippery sea-scavenger, cruising off to starboard of a ship bound for Tarshish, Spain, the western boundary of the then-known world, waiting for his promised dinner.

Dinner? Well, not quite, for the main item on the menu, Jonah, was only a morsel intended to be tasted and kept in storage, rather than one to be chewed and digested.

Scene 1. The fish cocks his slippery ear. What a commotion on board! A sudden storm had blown up and was threatening to reduce the ship to narrow gauge driftwood. Sailors and passengers seemed to be vying for the distinction of throwing the greatest quantity of their own and the ship's goods overboard to lighten the load. Voyagers ran this way and that, jostling each other in their confusion.

All were frantic—except for one landlubber who lay peacefully snoring down in the hold. He awoke to a strong hand dealing him a rough shaking. It was the ship's master.

"How can you sleep at a time like this? The ship is about to go down! Get up and call on your God to help us!"

Jonah rubbed his eyes. He made an effort to get up, but a quick lurch of the ship threw him back into his bunk.

Meanwhile, on the upper deck, the ship's hands were casting lots, as was the common practice in those days, to see who was responsible for this unnatural, overgrown thundersquall. The lot fell to Jonah.

Poking his head up through the hatch, Jonah was met by an angry mob.

"Why?" one of the men demanded, "why have you done this?"

Jonah knew only too well. "I was running away. God ordered

me to go to Nineveh and warn them that unless they turn from their wicked ways, His punishment will fall on them.

"Nineveh!" one of the deck hands snorted, pointing over the stern, "That's back there!"

"I know," Jonah replied, a little sadly.

Nineveh, a city of over half a million, was the capital of the heathen world. Jonah was a Jew. The idea of preaching repentance to a heathen nation was most repugnant. Jonah thought only the Jews should be God's people. And besides, Nineveh was the enemy of his nation, and he was not about to help his nation's enemy.

A piece of sail, torn by the fury of the winds, dealt the runaway prophet a wet slap across the face. The sea flung itself at the cringing craft like a raging beast.

"What are we going to do with this renegade?" one of the mates demanded anxiously. "We'll all drown!"

With a roar like a mighty waterfall, an enormous wave surged over the rail, sending several men sprawling.

"Take me," Jonah ordered, "and throw me overboard. There's no use all of you losing your lives."

But no man laid hands on him.

In a last effort, the men on the oars pulled until their muscles cried out, but they could not bring the vessel to shore.

There was nothing else to do. With a heave ho, they pitched Jonah out. And the storm lifted.

This is where the fish took over.

For three days and three nights Jonah rolled around in the sea monster's interior, begging God's mercy. God heard, and ordered the fish to heave up its passenger on the shore. The fish's part of the drama was now ended; Jonah still had several more scenes to play.

Scene 2. God speaks to Jonah a second time: "Go to Nineveh."

This time Jonah went. For three or four days he traveled throughout the city of Nineveh preaching: "In forty days this great beehive of humanity will be destroyed—unless you turn from your wickedness to God."

The people listened and determined to change their ways. Proclaiming a fast, they dressed themselves and all their household animals in sackcloth and ashes, from the king on down to the least in the kingdom.

"Let us all cry mightily unto God," proclaimed the king, "and turn from our evil ways. Who can tell if God will turn and repent and spare us from His fierce anger."

God did see their repentant hearts and spared them. The people had listened to Jonah's warning   Jonah was happy? See Scene 3.

Scene 3. Jonah is so angry, he could demolish Nineveh all by himself. He pours out his wrath to God: "You sent me to tell Nineveh it would be annihilated. Now you aren't even going to hurt one hair of it! The people of Nineveh are wicked and they should be punished! I can't stand it! If You aren't going to kill them, I wish you'd kill me!"

Peeved and pouting, Jonah stomped out of the city and sat down to wait for its complete destruction.

And lo, God made a gourd vine to spring up and cool Jonah in its shade. Jonah rejoiced.

But God also prepared a worm, and the next morning before the sun was scarcely peeking over the horizon, the worm gnawed through the vine, and it withered.

It turned out to be a hot day. A scorching east wind and the blistering sun brought Jonah again to the point of desperation. "If only I could die!"

"Jonah!" the Lord called. "Are you angry about the gourd?"

Jonah did not need to answer.

"You pity the gourd, you pity yourself," God went on, "and yet you have not one smidgen of pity for the city of Nineveh with its 120,000 small children? You would have Me slay them, even after the people have changed their ways?"

There was nothing left for Jonah to say. Had his friend the fish still been around, he might have gladly climbed in. Only this time he wouldn't have needed a briny beast of such magnitude. Jonah felt very small.

Jonah

CHAPTER 1

THE LORD SENT this message to Jonah, the son of Amittai:

2 "Go to the great city of Nineveh, and give them this announcement from the Lord: 'I am going to destroy you, for your wickedness rises before Me; it smells to highest heaven.'"

3 But Jonah was afraid to go and ran away from the Lord. He went down to the seacoast, to the port of Joppa, where he found a ship leaving for Tarshish. He bought a ticket, went on board, and climbed down into the dark hold of the ship to hide there from the Lord.

4 But as the ship was sailing along, suddenly the Lord flung a terrific wind over the sea, causing a great storm that threatened to send them to the bottom.

5-7 Fearing for their lives, the desperate sailors shouted to their gods for help and threw the cargo overboard to lighten the ship. And all this time Jonah was sound asleep down in the hold. So the captain went down after him. "What do you mean," he roared, "sleeping at a time like this? Get up and cry to your god, and see if he will have mercy on us and save us!" Then the crew decided to draw straws to see which of them had offended the gods and caused this terrible storm; and Jonah drew the short one.

8 "What have you done," they asked, "to bring this awful storm upon us? Who are you? What is your work? What country are you from? What is your nationality?"

9-11 And he said, "I am a Jew;[1] I worship Jehovah, the God of heaven, who made the earth and sea." Then he told them he was running away from the Lord. The men were terribly frightened when they heard this. "Oh, why did you do it?" they shouted; "What should we do to you to stop the storm?" For it was getting worse and worse.

12-13 "Throw me out into the sea," he said, "and it will become calm again. For I know this terrible storm has come

[1]Literally, "a Hebrew."

because of me." They tried harder to row the boat ashore, but couldn't make it. The storm was too fierce to fight against.

14-16 Then they shouted out a prayer to Jehovah, Jonah's God. "Oh Jehovah," they pleaded, "don't make us die for this man's sin; and don't hold us responsible for his death, for it is not our fault—You have sent this storm upon him for Your own good reasons." Then they picked up Jonah and threw him overboard into the raging sea—and the storm stopped! The men stood there in awe before Jehovah, and sacrificed to Him and vowed to serve Him.

17 Now the Lord had arranged for a huge fish to swallow Jonah. And Jonah was inside the fish three days and three nights.

CHAPTER 2

THEN JONAH PRAYED to the Lord his God from inside the fish:

2-4 "In my great trouble I cried to the Lord and He answered me; from the depths of death I called, and, Lord, You heard me! You threw me into the ocean depths; I sank down into the floods of waters and was covered by Your wild and stormy waves. Then I said, 'Oh Lord, You have rejected me and cast me away. How shall I ever again see Your holy temple?'

5-8 "I sank beneath the waves, and death was very near. The waters closed above me; the seaweed wrapped itself around my head. I went down to the bottoms of the mountains that rise from off the ocean floor. I was locked out of life and imprisoned in the land of death. But, oh Lord my God, You have snatched me from the yawning jaws of death! When I had lost all hope, I turned my thoughts once more to the Lord. And my earnest prayer went to You in Your holy temple. (Those who worship false gods have turned their backs on all the mercies waiting for them from the Lord!)

9 "I will never worship anyone but You! For how can I thank You enough for all You have done? I will surely fulfill my promises. For my deliverance comes from the Lord alone."

10 And the Lord ordered the fish to spit up Jonah on to the beach, and it did.

CHAPTER 3

THEN THE LORD SPOKE to Jonah again: "Go to that

great city, Nineveh," He said, "and warn them of their doom, as I told you to before!"

3 So Jonah obeyed, and went to Nineveh. Now Nineveh was a very large city, with extensive suburbs—so large that it would take three days to walk around it.[1]

4-5 The very first day when Jonah entered the city and began to preach, the people repented. Jonah shouted to the crowds that gathered around him, "Forty days from now Nineveh will be destroyed!" And they believed him and declared a fast; from the king on down everyone put on sackcloth—the rough, coarse garments worn at times of mourning.[2]

6-9 For when the king of Nineveh heard what Jonah was saying, he stepped down from his throne and laid aside his royal robes and put on sackcloth and sat in ashes. And the king and his nobles sent this message throughout the city: "Let no one, not even the animals, eat anything at all, nor even drink any water. Everyone must wear sackcloth and cry mightily to God; and let everyone turn from his evil ways, from his violence and robbing. Who can tell? Perhaps even yet God will decide to let us live, and will hold back His fierce anger from destroying us."

10 And when God saw that they had put a stop to their evil ways, He abandoned His plan to destroy them, and didn't carry it through.

CHAPTER 4

THIS CHANGE OF PLANS made Jonah very angry.

2-3 He complained to the Lord about it: "This is exactly what I thought You'd do, Lord, when I was there in my own country and You first told me to come here. That's why I ran away to Tarshish. For I knew You were a gracious God, merciful, slow to get angry, and full of kindness; I knew how easily You could cancel Your plans for destroying these people. Please kill me, Lord; I'd rather be dead than alive (when nothing that I told them happens[2])."

4 Then the Lord said, "Is it right to be *angry* about *this?*"

5-6 So Jonah went out and sat sulking[2] on the east side of the city, and he made a leafy shelter to shade him as he waited there

---

[1]The Hebrew text makes no distinction between the city proper—the walls of which were only about 8 miles in circumference, accommodating a population of about 175,000 persons—and the administrative district of Nineveh which was about 30-60 miles across.
[2]Implied.

to see if anything would happen to the city. And when the leaves of the shelter withered in the heat, the Lord arranged for a vine to grow up quickly and spread its broad leaves over Jonah's head to shade him. This made him comfortable and very grateful.

7-8 But God also prepared a worm! The next morning the worm ate through the stem of the plant, so that it withered away and died. Then, when the sun was hot, God ordered a scorching east wind to blow on Jonah, and the sun beat down upon his head until he grew faint and wished to die. For he said, "Death is better than this!"

9 And God said to Jonah, "Is it right for you to be angry because the plant died?" "Yes," Jonah said, "it is; it is right for me to be angry enough to die!"

10-11 Then the Lord said, "You feel sorry for yourself when your shelter is destroyed, though you did no work to put it there, and it is, at best, short-lived. And why shouldn't I feel sorry for a great city like Nineveh with its 120,000 people in utter spiritual darkness, and all its cattle?"

Maybe the Minor Prophets were under 21 . . .
but I didn't find any lollipops

Bold Journey—
B. C. Style

Micah THREW TOGETHER the few necessary travel items—a goatskin to carry water, a slab of salt-cured fish, several pounds of dates, his rough woolen robe which would serve as his coat by day and his blanket and mattress by night—and set off on foot for a dusty speaking tour of the country.

He didn't mind so much the long, hot walk, or making the speeches; crowds seemed to form naturally whenever they heard that he was going to bring a message from God, but once they got the drift of what he was saying . . .

Actually he wasn't presenting very popular stuff. Instead of a sweet, syrupy type of entertainment, Micah was tossing out remarks like: "You lie awake nights scheming how to get your neighbor's possessions—his fields and flocks and houses and barns and wife—then you get up in the morning and do him out of them. You hate what is good and love what is evil. And you who are leaders are even worse; you treat the people as though they were animals for you to slaughter."

At this point in the address, a few of the listeners were bent over double—not with laughter, but for gathering suitable stones with which to pummel this offensive fellow. But Micah went right on:

"Watch out! God will come down and trample you underfoot, you who take widows' homes away from them to make yourselves richer, you who push orphans out to wander the streets because you are too selfish to share some of your great wealth with them!"

Suddenly a man in the back of the crowd raised a stone above his shoulder and took aim. Seeing him, Micah snatched up his

65

few belongings from the ground and darted out of the crowd, out of town, and down the road toward the next one-night stand.

Too bad, he mused when he had shaken loose from the crowd, that the people hadn't let him stay long enough to deliver the rest of the message—it had a bangup finish (and one of these days he was almost certain to find himself in a town without rocks). He rehearsed it as he hiked along:

"Out of the little village of Bethlehem will come a great leader for Israel, one who has been from old, even from everlasting." The promise that the Savior would come! Micah wondered when the great day of the Savior's appearance would be. Perhaps in *his* lifetime? Oh, to live to see him!

As he trudged along through the dust, he thought about the other prophecy that God had given him to tell the people, that the day would come when the house of the Lord would be established, and people would flock toward it, people of all nations gathering to sing praises to God.

Overhead a silent-winged bird soared into the darkening sky. The moon was rising; the first stars were beginning to appear above the Judean hillside. Micah would have to hurry to reach the next little village before darkness engulfed the land.

He wondered what sort of an audience he would find the next day, and if they would pick up stones. But the stones were of little concern compared to the message. Would they listen to his message, or would they harden their hearts? Oh, that they would listen and turn again to God!

Micah

CHAPTER 1

THESE ARE MESSAGES from the Lord to Micah, who lived in the town of Moresheth during the reigns of King Jotham, King Ahaz and King Hezekiah, all kings of Judah. The messages were addressed to both Samaria and Judah, and came to Micah in the form of visions.

2-4 Attention! Let all the peoples of the world listen. For the Lord in His holy temple has made accusations against you! Look! He is coming! He leaves His throne in heaven and comes to earth, walking on the mountain tops. They melt beneath His feet, and flow into the valleys like wax in fire, like water pouring down a hill.

5 And why is this happening? Because of the sins of Israel and Judah. What sins? The idolatry and oppression centering in the capital cities, Samaria and Jerusalem!

6-7 Therefore the entire city of Samaria will crumble into a heap of rubble, and become an open field, her streets plowed up for planting grapes! The Lord will tear down her wall and her forts exposing their foundations, and pour their stones into the valleys below. All her carved images will be smashed to pieces; her ornate idol temples, built with the gifts of worshipers, will all be burned.[1]

8-9 I will wail and lament, howling as a jackal, mournful as an ostrich crying across the desert sands at night. I will walk naked and barefoot in sorrow and shame; for my people's wound is far too deep to heal. The Lord stands ready at Jerusalem's gates to punish her.

10 Woe to the city of Gath. Weep, men of Bakah. In Beth-le-Aphrah roll in the dust in your anguish and shame.

11 There go the people of Shaphir[2], led away as slaves— stripped, naked and ashamed. The people of Zaanan[2] dare not

---

[1]Literally, "they shall return to the hire of an harlot."

[2]In the Hebrew, there is frequent word play in verses 10-14. Micah bitterly declaims each town, demonstrating by the use of puns their failures. *Shaphir* sounds like the Hebrew word for "beauty," here contrasted with their shame; *Zaanan* sounds like a verb meaning "to go forth," here contrasted with the fear of its inhabitants to venture outside; *Beth-ezel* sounds like a word for "foundation," which has been taken away from them.

show themselves outside their walls. The foundations of Beth-ezel[2] are swept away—the very ground on which it stood.

12 The people of Maroth vainly hope for better days, but only bitterness awaits them as the Lord stands poised against Jerusalem.

13 Quick! Use your swiftest chariots and flee, oh people of Lachish, for you were the first of the cities of Judah to follow Israel in her sin of idol worship. Then all the cities of the south began to follow your example.

14 Write off Moresheth[3] of Gath; there is no hope of saving her. The town of Achzib has deceived the kings of Israel, for she promised help she cannot give.

15-16 You people of Mareshah will be a prize to your enemies. They will penetrate to Adullum, the "Pride of Israel." Weep, weep for your little ones. For they are snatched away and you will never see them again. They have gone as slaves to distant lands. Shave your heads in sorrow.

CHAPTER 2

WOE TO YOU who lie awake at night, plotting wickedness; you rise at dawn to carry out your schemes; because you can, you do.

2 You want a certain piece of land, or someone else's house (though it is all he has); you take it by fraud and threats and violence.

3-5 But the Lord God says, I will reward your evil with evil; nothing can stop Me; never again will you be proud and haughty after I am through with you. Then your enemies will taunt you and mock your dirge of despair: "We are finished, ruined. God has confiscated our land and sent us far away, and given what is ours to others." Others will set your boundaries then. "The People of the Lord" will live where they are sent.

6-9 "Don't say such things," the people say. "Don't harp on things like that. It's disgraceful, that sort of talk. Such evils surely will not come our way." Is that the right reply for you to make, O

[2]In the Hebrew, there is frequent word play in verses 10-14. Micah bitterly declaims each town, demonstrating by the use of puns their failures. *Shaphir* sounds like the Hebrew word for "beauty," here contrasted with their shame; *Zaanan* sounds like a verb meaning "to go forth," here contrasted with the fear of its inhabitants to venture outside; *Beth-ezel* sounds like a word for "foundation," which has been taken away from them.
[3]Micah's home town. See verse 1 of chapter 1.

House of Jacob? Do you think the Spirit of the Lord likes to talk to you so roughly? No! His threats are for your good, to get you on the path again. Yet to this very hour My people rise against Me. For you steal the shirts right off the backs of those who trusted you, who walk in peace. You have driven out the widows from their homes, and stripped their children of every God-given right.

10-11 Up! Begone! This is no more your land and home; for you have filled it with sin and it will vomit you out. "I'll preach to you the joys of wine and drink"—that is the kind of drunken, lying prophet that you like!

12-13 The time will come, O Israel, when I will gather you— all that are left—and bring you together again like sheep in a fold, like a flock in a pasture—a noisy, happy crowd. The Messiah[1] will lead you out of exile and bring you through the gates of your cities of captivity, back to your own land. Your King will go before you—the Lord leads on.

CHAPTER 3

Listen, YOU LEADERS OF ISRAEL—you are supposed to know right from wrong,

2-4 Yet you are the very ones who hate good and love evil; you skin My people and strip them to the bone. You devour them, flog them, break their bones, and chop them up like meat for the cooking pot—and then you plead with the Lord for His help in times of trouble! Do you really expect Him to listen? He will look the other way!

5-7 You false prophets! You who lead His people astray! You who cry "Peace" to those who give you food, and threaten those who will not pay! This is God's message to you: The night will close about you and cut off all your visions; darkness will cover you, with never a word from God. The sun will go down upon you and your day will end. Then at last you will cover your faces in shame, and admit that your messages were not from God.

8-12 But as for me, I am filled with power, with the Spirit of the Lord, fearlessly announcing God's punishment on Israel for her sins. Listen to me, you leaders of Israel who hate justice and love unfairness, and fill Jerusalem with murder and sin of every kind—you leaders who take bribes; you priests and prophets

[1]"He who opens the breach."

who won't preach and prophesy until you're paid: (And yet you fawn upon the Lord and say, "All is well—the Lord is here among us. No harm can come to us.") It is because of you that Jerusalem will be plowed like a field, and become a heap of rubble; the mountaintop where the temple stands will be overgrown with brush.

CHAPTER 4

BUT IN THE LAST DAYS Mount Zion will be the most renowned of all the mountains of the world, praised by all nations; people from all over the world will make pilgrimages there.

2-5 "Come," they will say to one another, "let us visit the mountain of the Lord, and see the temple of the God of Israel; He will tell us what to do, and we will do it."

For in those days the whole world will be ruled by the Lord from Jerusalem! He will issue His laws and announce His decrees from there. He will arbitrate among the nations and dictate to strong nations far away. They will beat their swords into plowshares and their spears into pruning-hooks; nations shall no longer fight each other, for all war will end. There will be universal peace, and all the military academies and training camps will be closed down. Everyone will live quietly in his own home in peace and prosperity, for there will be nothing to fear. The Lord Himself has promised this. (Therefore we will follow the Lord our God forever and ever, even though all the nations around us worship idols!)

6-8 In that coming day, the Lord says that He will bring back His punished people—sick and lame and dispossessed—and make them strong again in their own land, a mighty nation; and the Lord Himself shall be their King from Mount Zion for ever. O Jerusalem—the Watchtower of God's people—your royal might and power will come back to you again, just as before.

9-10 But for now, now you scream in terror. Where is your king to lead you? He is dead! Where are your wise men? All are gone! Pain has gripped you like a woman in travail. Writhe and groan in your terrible pain, oh people of Zion; for you must leave this city and live in the fields; you will be sent far away into exile in Babylon. But there I will rescue you and free you from the grip of your enemies.

11-13 True, many nations have gathered together against you, calling for your blood, eager to destroy you. But they do not know My thoughts nor understand My plan; for the time will come when the Lord will gather together the enemies of His people like sheaves upon the threshing floor, helpless before Israel. Rise, thresh, O daughter of Zion; I will give you horns of iron and hoofs of brass and you will trample to pieces many people; and you will give their wealth as offerings to the Lord, the Lord of all the earth.

CHAPTER 5

MOBILIZE! The enemy lays siege to Jerusalem! With a rod they shall strike the Judge of Israel on the face.

2-3 O Bethlehem Ephrathah, you are but a small Judean village, yet you will be the birthplace of My King who is alive from everlasting ages past! God will abandon His people to their enemies until the time of Israel's spiritual rebirth;[1] then at last the exiled remnants of Israel will rejoin their brethren in their own land.

4-6 And He shall stand and feed His flock in the strength of the Lord, in the majesty of the Name of the Lord His God; and His people shall remain there undisturbed, for He will be greatly honored all around the world. He will be our Peace. And when the Assyrian invades our land and marches across our hills, He will appoint seven shepherds to watch over us, eight princes to lead us. They will rule Assyria with drawn swords and enter the gates of the land of Nimrod. He will deliver us from the Assyrians when they invade our land.

7-14 Then the nation of Israel will refresh the world like a gentle dew or the welcome showers of rain, and Israel will be as strong as a lion. The nations will be like helpless sheep before her! She will stand up to her foes; all her enemies will be wiped out. At that same time, says the Lord, I will destroy all the weapons you depend on, and tear down your walls and demolish the defenses of your cities. I will put an end to all witchcraft—there will be no more fortune-tellers to consult; and destroy all your idols—never again will you worship what you have made; and I will abolish the heathen shrines from among you, and destroy the cities where your idol temples stand.

[1]Literally, "until she who is in travail has brought forth."

71

15 And I will pour out My vengeance upon the nations who refuse to obey Me.

CHAPTER 6

LISTEN TO WHAT THE LORD IS SAYING to His people: Stand up and state your case against Me. Let the mountains and hills be called to witness your complaint.

2 And now, O mountains, listen to the Lord's complaint! For He has a case against His people Israel! He will prosecute them to the full.

3-5 O My people, what have I done that makes you turn away from Me? Tell Me why your patience is exhausted! Answer Me! For I brought you out of Egypt, and cut your chains of slavery; and I gave you Moses, Aaron, and Miriam to help you. Don't you remember, O My people, how Balak, king of Moab, tried to destroy you through the curse of Balaam, son of Beor, but I made him bless you instead? That is the kindness I showed you again and again. Have you no memory at all of what happened at Acacia and Gilgal, and how I blessed you there?

6-8 "How can we make up to You for what we've done?" you ask. "Shall we bow before the Lord with offerings of yearling calves?" Oh, no! For if you offered Him thousands of rams and ten thousands of rivers of olive oil—would that please Him? Would He be satisfied? If you sacrificed your oldest child, would that make Him glad? Then would He forgive your sins? Of course not! No, He has told you what He wants, and this is all it is: to be fair and just and merciful, and to walk humbly with your God.

9-13 The Lord's voice calls out to all Jerusalem—listen to the Lord if you are wise! The armies of destruction are coming; the Lord is sending them. For your sins are very great—is there to be no end of getting rich by cheating? The homes of the wicked are full of ungodly treasures and lying scales. Shall I say "Good!" to all your merchants with their bags of false, deceitful weights? How could God be just while saying that? Your rich men are wealthy through extortion and violence; your citizens are so used to lying that their tongues can't tell the truth! Therefore I will wound you! I will make your hearts miserable for all your sins.

14-16 You will eat but never have enough; hunger pangs and emptiness will still remain. And though you try and try to save

72

your money, it will come to nothing at the end; and what little you succeed in storing up I'll give to those who conquer you![1] You will plant crops but not harvest them; you will press out the oil from the olives, and not get enough to anoint yourself! You will trample the grapes, but get no juice to make your wine. The only commands you keep are those of Omri; the only example you follow is that of Ahab! Therefore I will make an awesome example of you—I will destroy you. I will make you the laughing-stock of the world; all who see you will snicker and sneer!

CHAPTER 7

WOE IS ME! It is as hard to find an honest man as it is to find the grapes and figs when harvest days are over. Not a cluster to eat, not a single early fig, however much I long for it! The good men have disappeared from the earth; not one fair-minded man is left. They are all murderers, turning against even their own brothers.

3-4 They go at their evil deeds with both hands; and how skilled they are in using them! The governor and judge alike demand bribes. The rich man pays them off and tells them whom to ruin. Justice is twisted between them. Even the best of them are prickly as briars; the straightest is more crooked than a hedge of thorns. But your judgment day is coming swiftly now; your time of punishment is almost here; confusion, destruction, and terror will be yours.

5-6 Don't trust anyone, not your best friend—not even your wife! For the son despises his father; the daughter defies her mother; the bride curses her mother-in-law. Yes, a man's enemies will be found in his own home.

7-8 As for me, I look to the Lord for His help; I wait for God to save me; He will hear me. Do not rejoice against me, oh my enemy; for though I fall, I will rise again! When I sit in darkness, the Lord Himself will be my Light.

9 I will be patient while the Lord punishes me, for I have sinned against Him; then He will defend me from my enemies, and punish them for all the evil they have done to me. God will bring me out of my darkness into the light, and I will see His goodness.

10 Then my enemy will see that God is for me, and be

[1]See Haggai 1:6.

ashamed for taunting me, "Where is that God of yours?" Now with my own eyes I see them trampled down like mud in the street.

11-12 Your cities, people of God, will be rebuilt, much larger and more prosperous than before. Citizens of many lands will come and honor you—from Assyria to Egypt, and from Egypt to the Euphrates, from sea to sea and from distant hills and mountains.

13 But first comes terrible destruction to Israel[1] for the great wickedness of her people.

14-17 O Lord, come and rule Your people; lead Your flock; make them live in peace and prosperity; let them enjoy the fertile pastures of Bashan and Gilead as they did long ago. "Yes," replies the Lord, "I will do mighty miracles for you, like those when I brought you out of slavery in Egypt. All the world will stand amazed at what I will do for you, and be embarrassed at their puny might. They will stand in silent awe, deaf to all around them." They will see what snakes they are, lowly as worms crawling from their holes. They will come trembling out from their fortresses to meet the Lord our God. They will fear Him; they will stand in awe.

18-20 Where is another God like You, who pardons the sins of the survivors among His people? You cannot stay angry with Your people, for You love to be merciful. Once again You will have compassion on us. You will tread our sins beneath Your feet; You will throw them into the depths of the ocean! You will bless us as You promised Jacob long ago. You will set Your love upon us, as You promised our father Abraham!

[1]Literally, "But the land will be desolate because of its inhabitants."

Minor Prophets? Sure,
I can name two or three of them . . . Hezekiah
. . . Melchizedek . . . Jehoshaphat . . .

The Wild West
Of The East

SEE THAT GHOST TOWN OVER THERE? That used to be Nineveh, one of the mightiest cities of the ancient East. Glittering, glamorous Nineveh—a metropolis of evil.

So powerful was Nineveh that she held many nations in slavery to pamper her whims. Little mattered to the people of Nineveh but their comfort and pleasure. Wickedness of every sort was taken for granted: lying, stealing, adultery, murder.

Finally, when the stench of her vanity and lies, her robberies and foulness became unbearable to God, He vowed that He would destroy the city utterly. And He did.

God didn't actually lift a finger against the city Himself; He just let it be known to the Medes and the Babylonians, Nineveh's enemies, that the Ninevites were so weakend by loose living that they could scarcely pick up a sword in their own defense.

The Medes and the Babylonians needed no further invitation. They hurriedly assembled armies and swept down on the city. A fearful sight in their bright red tunics and shields, the marauders raced through the streets in their chariots, here setting homes afire, there cutting down the people with swords and spears.

On charged the charioteers through the city, waving lighted torches and slinging them when they saw a likely target.

The city was large, but so was the army, and after they had massacred the populace and scooped up all the valuables, they committed their final act against the city: they opened the gates of the dam that protected Nineveh. With a mighty roar, the waters of the Tigris surged in. Buildings toppled beneath the onrush, and the silt and sand borne by the water filled the spaces in between. The destruction of Nineveh was complete.

When the waters receded, only an occasional stone or clump of bricks protruded from the rolling acres of sand to hint that there had once been a mighty city there. So thoroughly was Nineveh wiped off the map that for centuries it was lost to the world. Only a few nomads and a handful of lions knew about it.

The lions, with just a little digging, made lairs among the ruins; birds lodged in the upper protrusions of the buildings. From afar off, wayfarers across that stretch of trackless expanse heard the growling and snarling of the lions and the weird crying of the cormorants and bitterns, and went out of their way to avoid the place.

As the years passed, Bible scholars began wondering where this city had been located. (The destruction of Nineveh took place about 600 years before Christ.) About the middle of the 19th Century, archeologists found the site.

As they worked, the city began to take shape—a house here, a stable there. Like a ghost town, Nineveh emerged from the sands. She stands today as a monument to the time God called a halt to the city's wickedness.

There was a prophet connected with the climactic episode in Nineveh's life. His name was Nahum, and he apparently lived in Galilee, the area where Jesus was to spend his boyhood some 600 years later. (Capernaum, 'village of Nahum' may have been named for him.)

Like Jonah, Nahum carried a message from God to Nineveh. But Jonah's message had been of grace. Nahum's foretold certain doom. For a century and a half since the time of Jonah, God had prolonged the day of mercy, but the time had come when He had to settle accounts with Nineveh.

God sent Nahum a vision of all the things that would happen. Nahum doesn't tell us whether he went and warned Nineveh, or simply wrote down what was to happen for the record. Perhaps God thought that Nineveh had had enough warnings. Jonah, after his spectacular journey to Nineveh by fish, had given the city plenty of warning, and the people had repented that time.

Anyway, Nineveh was finally destroyed, just as God told Nahum it would be.

Nineveh, Wild West of the East, was so totally wiped out that she had to be dug up to even become a ghost town. It's like the cowboys say in the westerns, "You're such an ornery, lowdown critter they'd have to dig you up to bury you!"

Nahum

THIS IS THE VISION God gave to Nahum, who lived in Elkosh, concerning the impending doom of Nineveh:[1]

2-5 God is jealous over those He loves; that is why He takes vengeance on those who hurt them. He furiously destroys their enemies. He is slow in getting angry, but when aroused His power is incredible, and He does not easily forgive. He shows His power in the terrors of the cyclone and the raging storms; clouds are billowing dust beneath His feet! At His command the oceans and rivers become dry sand; the lush pastures of Bashan and Carmel fade away; the green forests of Lebanon wilt. In His presence mountains quake and hills melt; the earth crumbles and its people are destroyed.

6-10 Who can stand before an angry God? His fury is like fire; the mountains tumble down before His anger. The Lord is good. When trouble comes, He is the place to go! And He knows everyone who trusts in Him! But He sweeps away His enemies with an overwhelming flood; He pursues them all night long. What are you thinking of, Nineveh, to defy the Lord? He will stop you with one blow; He won't need to strike again. He tosses His enemies into the fire like a tangled mass of thorns. They burst into flames like straw.

11-12 Who is this king[2] of yours who dares to plot against the Lord? But the Lord is not afraid of him! "Though he build his army millions strong," the Lord declares, "it will vanish. O My people, I have punished you enough!

13-14 "Now I will break your chains and release you from the yoke of slavery to this Assyrian king."[2] And to the king He says, "I have ordered an end to your dynasty; your sons will never sit upon your throne. And I will destroy your gods and temples, and I will bury you! For how you stink with sin!"

15 See, the messengers come running down the mountains with glad news: "The invaders have been wiped out and we are safe!" O Judah, proclaim a day of thanksgiving, and worship only the Lord, as you have vowed. For this enemy from Nineveh

[1]Nineveh was the Assyrian capital.
[2]Implied from verse 1 and 3:18.

will never come again. He is cut off forever; he will never be seen again.

CHAPTER 2

NINEVEH, YOU ARE FINISHED![1] You are already surrounded by enemy armies! Sound the alarm! Man the ramparts! Muster your defenses, full force, and keep a sharp watch for the enemy attack to begin!

2 For the land of the people of God lies empty and broken after your attacks but the Lord will restore their honor and power again!

3-4 Shields flash red in the sunlight! The attack begins! See their scarlet uniforms! See their glittering chariots moving forward side by side, pulled by prancing steeds! Your own chariots race recklessly along the streets and through the squares, darting like lightning, gleaming like torches.

5-6 The king shouts for his officers; they stumble in their haste, rushing to the walls to set up their defenses. But too late! The river gates are open! The enemy has entered! The palace is in panic!

7-10 The queen of Nineveh is brought out naked to the streets, and led away, a slave, with all her maidens weeping after her; listen to them mourn like doves, and beat their breasts! Nineveh is like a leaking water tank! Her soldiers slip away, deserting her; she cannot hold them back. "Stop, stop," she shouts, but they keep on running. Loot the silver! Loot the gold! There seems to be no end of treasures. Her vast, uncounted wealth is stripped away. Soon the city is an empty shambles; hearts melt in horror; knees quake; her people stand aghast, palefaced and trembling.

11-13 Where now is that great Nineveh, lion of the nations, full of fight and boldness, where even the old and feeble, as well as the young and tender, lived unafraid? Oh, Nineveh, once mighty lion! You crushed your enemies to feed your children and your wives, and filled your city and your homes with captured goods and slaves. But now the Lord of hosts has turned against you. He destroys your weapons. Your chariots stand there, silent and unused. Your finest youth lie dead. Never again will you

[1]This chapter predicts the events of the year 612 B.C., when the combined armies of the Babylonians and Medes sacked impregnable Nineveh.

bring back slaves from conquered nations; never again will you rule the earth.

CHAPTER 3

WOE TO NINEVEH, City of Blood, full of lies, crammed with plunder.

2 Listen! Hear the crack of the whips as the chariots rush forward against her; wheels rumbling, horses' hoofs pounding, and chariots clattering as they bump wildly through the streets!

3-7 See the flashing swords and glittering spears in the upraised arms of the cavalry! The dead are lying in the streets—bodies, heaps of bodies, everywhere. Men stumble over them, scramble to their feet, and fall again. All this because Nineveh sold herself to the enemies of God. The beautiful and faithless city, mistress of deadly charms, enticed the nations with her beauty, then taught them all to worship her false gods,[1] bewitching people everywhere. "No wonder I stand against you," says the Lord of Hosts; "and now all the earth will see your nakedness and shame. I will cover you with filth and show the world how really vile you are." All who see you will shrink back in horror: "Nineveh lies in utter ruin." Yet no one anywhere regrets your fate!

8-13 Are you any better than Thebes,[2] straddling the Nile, protected on all sides by the River? Ethiopia and the whole land of Egypt were her mighty allies; and she could call on them for infinite assistance, as well as Put and Libya. Yet Thebes fell and her people were led off as slaves; her babies were dashed to death against the stones of the streets. Soldiers drew straws to see who would get her officers as servants. All her leaders were bound in chains. Nineveh, too, will stagger like a drunkard and hide herself in fear. All your forts will fall. They will be devoured like first-ripe figs that fall into the mouths of those who shake the trees. Your troops will be weak and helpless as women. The gates of your land will be opened wide to the enemy and set on fire and burned.

14-17 Get ready for the siege! Store up water! Strengthen the forts! Prepare many bricks for repairing your walls! Go into the pits to trample the clay, and pack it in the molds! But in the middle of your preparations, the fire will devour you; the sword

[1]Literally, "who betrays nations with her harlotries."
[2]Thebes was conquered by the Assyrians 51 years before this prophecy.

will cut you down; the enemy will consume you like young locusts that eat up everything before them. There is no escape, though you multiply like grasshoppers. Merchants, numerous as stars, filled your city with vast wealth, but your enemies swarm like locusts and carry it away. Your princes and officials crowd together like grasshoppers in the hedges in the cold; but all of them will flee away and disappear, like locusts when the sun comes up and warms the earth.

18-19   O Assyrian king, your princes lie dead in the dust; your people are scattered across the mountains; there is no shepherd now to gather them. There is no healing for your wound—it is far too deep to cure. All who hear your fate will clap their hands for joy; for where can one be found who has not suffered from your cruelty?

Nobody reads the Minor Prophets.
They weren't with it—even 2,000 years ago!

Habakkuk: Tower Sitter

HABAKKUK THE PROPHET, up in the tower of his vineyard watching for thieves (it was nearly harvest time and the vines were heavy with tempting grapes), stamped his feet and fumed. The more he thought about it, the angrier he got.

He was angry with God—angry because the wicked people of the land were oppressing others unmercifully, and God was letting them do it.

Habakkuk could no longer stand to watch those in power committing violence of every sort. They cheated the people in business transactions every chance they got, robbed them of what little they had, lied about them and got them into trouble, even murdered them if it furthered their own plans. It was getting so that people expected life to be nothing but suffering.

And the wicked, wealthy, powerful ones could do all this without fear of punishment—no longer were the laws of the land enforced. Law cases were scheduled, but never came to trial—or, if they did, the decision was sure to favor those in power.

And so the wicked went their merry way, scoffing at God, worshiping idols, not missing any opportunity to take advantage of the common people.

Habakkuk just couldn't stand it any longer.

He opened his mouth and cried out in a loud voice to God, "How long will You let this go on? Can't You see what the wicked are doing? Why don't You put an end to this violence?"

The situation was so rotten that Habakkuk half expected that God must have gone off somewhere and retired, no longer paying any attention to what was happening on earth.

He was a little startled therefore when he heard God answering:

"Don't worry, Habakkuk. Before long I'm going to give the wicked what they deserve—and in such a way that you'll hardly believe it. You know the Chaldeans . . . "

Habakkuk nodded. He knew the Chaldeans. In all the world there was not a nation fiercer or more terrible than the Chaldeans. The Chaldean horsemen were swifter than leopards, more vicious than the wolves that prowled the hills at night. The very mention of the word Chaldeans was enough to strike terror into the heart of the bravest man.

"At my leading," God went on, "the Chaldean horsemen will come down upon the country with one goal in mind: violence. Like eagles they will sweep across the countryside; like famished eagles they will devour everything in their path."

A chill ran down Habakkuk's backbone. He was going to make sure he was out of the way when the Chaldeans came!

"Just a minute!" God put in. "Before you settle down in your tower, I want you to write down these things I have told you. Write them plainly on tablets and show them to all the people. The righteous will read and know that I am true to my word, and will run to escape the destruction. The righteous man trusts in Me—and lives!"

What about the wicked, those who have no faith in God's promises? "The wicked will not be interested in reading a message from Me," God went on. "They will laugh at what I say I am going to do, and while they are still laughing, they will be destroyed."

"When will all this happen?" Habakkuk wanted to know.

"At the appointed time," God assured him. "Wait for it. It will come."

So Habakkuk prepared the tablets and set them up in the marketplace where all could read them.

Some townspeople read the proclamation, gathered up their belongings, and hurried out of town. The unbelievers, laughing and scoffing at the frightened believers scurrying out of the city, remained.

Reaching the top of his tower, Habakkuk looked out over the beautiful land that rolled gently to the south, groves of olive trees dotting the landscape. To the north the hills rose more steeply, the horizon crowned with the hazy peaks of a distant mountain range.

How, Habbkuk marveled, could men here in God's creation

live lives vile beyond description? If only they knew God.

Then one day, as Habakkuk looked out from his tower, the Chaldeans came, racing across the countryside—a fearful sight on their frenzied horses. They broke into homes, grabbed everything of value, murdered the people and burned the buildings after them. Racing from house to house, they slaughtered and stole and set fires.

Never, even in his wildest imagination, had Habakkuk seen or heard of anything so ferocious.

The valley below him was a mass of flames and smoke now. Habakkuk plugged his ears to shut out the wailing of the victims, and at the same time tried to keep from inhaling the smoke that curled up into his tower. As he watched, the fury of the Chaldeans seemed to be increasing. On and on they rode, devastating every part of the broad valley. Habakkuk knew that no one could survive such an onslaught. He only hoped the attackers would pass by far below without noticing his tower.

Then gradually the smoke cleared away and the invaders were gone. The valley lay in burned-out ruin, a wasteland devoid of people. Habakkuk remembered how he had cried to God to do something about the wicked, and how God had said He would destroy them in such a way that Habakkuk would hardly believe it.

God had done it. He had wiped out the wicked and spared His own, once more encouraging His people to walk in His way, once more encouraging them to live by faith.

"The righteous man trusts in Me—and lives!" Habakkuk repeated to himself as he climbed down from his tower. "The righteous man trusts in Me—and lives!"

Habakkuk

THIS IS THE MESSAGE that came to the prophet Habakkuk in a vision from God:

2-4 O Lord, how long must I call for help before You will listen? I shout to You in vain; there is no answer. "Help! Murder!" I cry, but no one comes to save. Must I forever see this sin and sadness all around me? Wherever I look there is oppression and bribery and men who love to argue and to fight. The law is not enforced and there is no justice given in the courts; for the wicked far outnumber the righteous, and bribes and trickery prevail.

5-11 The Lord replied: "Look! and be amazed! You will be astounded at what I am about to do! For I am going to do something in your own lifetime that you will have to see to believe. I am raising a new force on the world scene, the Chaldeans,[1] a cruel and violent nation who will march across the world and conquer it. They are notorious for their cruelty. They do as they like, and no one can interfere. Their horses are swifter than leopards. They are a fierce people, more fierce than wolves at dusk. Their cavalry move proudly forward from a distant land; like eagles they come swooping down to pounce upon their prey. All opposition melts away before the terror of their presence. They collect captives like sand. They scoff at kings and princes, and scorn their forts. They simply heap up dirt against their walls and capture them! They sweep past like wind and are gone; but their guilt is deep, for they claim their power is from their gods."[2]

12-13 O Lord my God, my Holy One, You who are Eternal— is Your plan in all of this to wipe us out? Surely not! O God our Rock, You have decreed the rise of these Chaldeans to chasten and correct us for our awful sins. We are wicked, but they far more! Will You, who cannot allow sin in any form, stand idly by

[1]Chaldeans: a tribe of Semites living between Babylon and the Persian Gulf, who began to assert themselves against the Assyrians around 630 BC, and 25 years later had mastered most of the Near East.
[2]The Hebrew text of this verse is very uncertain.

86

while they swallow us up? Should You be silent while the wicked destroy those who are better than they?

14-16 Are we but fish, to be caught and killed? Are we but creeping things that have no leader to defend them from their foes? Must we be strung up on their hooks and dragged out in their nets, while they rejoice? Then they will worship their nets! and burn incense before them! "These are the gods who make us rich," they'll say.

17 Will You let them get away with this forever? Will they succeed forever in their heartless wars?

CHAPTER 2

I WILL CLIMB MY WATCHTOWER NOW, and wait to see what answer God will give to my complaint.

* * * *

2-4 And the Lord said to me, "Write My answer on a billboard,[1] large and clear, so that anyone can read it at a glance and rush to tell the others. But these things I plan won't happen right away. Slowly, steadily, surely, the time approaches when the vision will be fulfilled. If it seems slow, do not despair, for these things will surely come to pass. Just be patient! They will not be overdue a single day! Note this: Wicked men trust themselves alone (as these Chaldeans do)[2]—and fail; but the righteous man trusts in Me—and lives![3]

5-6 What's more, these arrogant Chaldeans are betrayed by all their wine, for it is treacherous. In their greed they have collected many nations, but like death and hell, they are never satisfied. The time is coming when all their captives will taunt them, saying: "You robbers! At last justice has caught up with you! Now you will get your just deserts for your oppression and extortion!"

7-8 Suddenly your debtors will rise up in anger and turn on you and take all you have, while you stand trembling and helpless. You have ruined many nations; now they will ruin you. You murderers! You have filled the countryside with lawlessness and all the cities too.

9-11 Woe to you for getting rich by evil means, attempting to live beyond the reach of danger. By the murders you commit, you

[1]Literally, "on the tablets."
[2]Implied.
[3]Or, "shall live by his faithfulness."

have shamed your name and forfeited your lives. The very stones in the walls of your homes cry out against you, and the beams in the ceilings echo what they say.

12-14 Woe to you who build cities with money gained from murdering and robbery! Has not the Lord decreed that godless nations' gains will turn to ashes in their hands? They work so hard, but all in vain! (The time will come when all the earth is filled, as the waters fill the sea, with an awareness of the glory of the Lord.)

15-18 Woe to you for making your neighboring lands reel and stagger like drunkards beneath your blows, and then gloating over their nakedness and shame. Soon your own glory will be replaced by shame. Drink down God's judgment on yourselves. Stagger and fall! You cut down the forests of Lebanon—now you will be cut down! You terrified the wild animals you caught in your traps—now terror will strike you because of all your murdering and violence in cities everywhere. What profit was there in worshiping all your man-made idols? What a foolish lie that they could help! What fools you were to trust what you yourselves had made.

19 Woe to those who command their lifeless wooden idols to arise and save them, who call out to the speechless stone to tell them what to do. Can images speak for God? They are overlaid with gold and silver, but there is no breath at all inside!

20 But the Lord is in His holy temple; let all the earth be silent before Him.

CHAPTER 3

THIS IS THE PRAYER OF TRIUMPH[1] *that Habakkuk sang before the Lord:*

2 O Lord, now I have heard Your report, and I worship You in awe for the fearful things You are going to do. In this time of our deep need, begin again to help us, as You die in years gone by. Show us Your power to save us. In Your wrath, remember mercy.

3-6 I see God moving across the deserts from Mount Sinai.[2] His brilliant splendor fills the earth and sky; His glory fills the heavens, and the earth is full of His praise! What a wonderful God He is! From His hands flash rays of brilliant light. He

[1]Literally, "according to Shigionoth"—thought by some to mean a mournful dirge.
[2]Literally, "from Teman . . . from Mount Paran."

rejoices[3] in His awesome power. Pestilence marches before Him; plague follows close behind. He stops; He stands still for a moment, gazing at the earth. Then He shakes the nations, scattering the everlasting mountains and leveling the hills. His power is just the same as always!

7-11 I see the people of Cushan and of Midian in mortal fear. [4]Was it in anger, Lord, You smote the rivers and parted the sea? Were You displeased with them? No, You were sending Your chariots of salvation! All saw Your power! Then springs burst forth upon the earth at Your command! The mountains watched and trembled. Onward swept the raging water. The mighty deep cried out, announcing its surrender to the Lord.[5] The lofty sun and moon began to fade, obscured by brilliance from Your arrows and the flashing of Your glittering spear.

12-15 You marched across the land in awesome anger, and trampled down the nations in Your wrath. You went out to save Your chosen people. You crushed the head of the wicked and laid bare his bones from head to toe. You destroyed with their own weapons those who came out like a whirlwind, thinking Israel would be an easy prey. Your horsemen marched across the sea; the mighty waters piled high.

16 I tremble when I hear all this; my lips quiver with fear. My legs give way beneath me and I shake in terror. I will quietly wait for the day of trouble to come upon the people who invade us.

*　　*　　*　　*

17-19 Even though the fig trees are all destroyed, and there is neither blossom left nor fruit; and though the olive crops all fail, and the fields lie barren; even if the flocks die in the fields and the cattle barns are empty, yet I will rejoice in the Lord; I will be happy in the God of my salvation. The Lord God is my Strength, and He will give me the speed of a deer and bring me safely over the mountains.

(A note to the choir director: When singing this ode, the choir is to be accompanied by stringed instruments.)

[3]Or, "He veils His power."
[4]Literally, "Was the Lord displeased against the rivers? Were you angry with them? Was your wrath against their sin that you rode upon your horses? Your chariots were salvation. Your bow was pulled from its sheath and you put arrows to the string. You ribboned the earth with rivers."
[5]Literally, "and lifts high its hands."

Who wants to be a prophet?
That takes a real square!

God Cleans
House

ZEPHANIAH THE PROPHET SHOOK HIS HEAD to clear the cobwebs out of his brain.

Had he heard right? Had God *really* said to him that He was going to destroy everyone? Everyone in all the land?

Zephaniah could hardly believe it. He knew that his was a wicked and unruly generation; people seemed to have reached an all-time low in low-downness. Surely no group anywhere had ever been more violent and depraved.

But destroy *everyone*! It didn't seem fair!

And why? Why would God destroy *everyone*? What about those who were faithful to Him? Certainly He wouldn't destroy *them*!

God had more to say: "I will slay *all* the people—not only those who worship idols, and those who have never sought Me, and those who have been Mine and have turned their backs on Me, but even those who worship Me."

Zephaniah was astounded! He could see why God might want to get rid of the wicked, but why would He do away with those who worshiped Him?

God explained: "Because those who worship Me are only half-hearted about it. They say, 'The Lord will not do good, neither will He do evil.' They go through the routine of worship without really believing that I am what I am. They're so lukewarm that they're not worth keeping alive."

"But—but—" Zephaniah pleaded, not wanting to see everyone perish, "if I went and told the people what you plan to do, perhaps they would come to their senses!"

"You can try. It may be that some will return to Me and I will be able to spare them."

That was all Zephaniah wanted to know. Without waiting for further instructions, he hurried out to warn the people. In little towns and big he gathered the people together and told them about the coming doom.

"We have turned away from God, and He is going to utterly destroy us all!" he warned. "He will leave no one alive! Our cities will become ruins on the desert. Not one of us will escape unless we return to Him!"

"He's a raving madman!" someone in the audience shouted.

"He's been cutting wheat in the hot sun too long!" someone else yelled. "It's scrambled his brain!"

The crowd laughed and jeered.

"A madman! A madman!" they chanted. "Get moving, madman. We don't want you around here!"

But a few listened. A few recognized the truth in his words, and a few, in their hearts, turned again to God.

God looked down and saw the few, and spoke again to Zephaniah: "I will save this remnant of the people. When I come to destroy the land, I will spare the lives of these few. From now on, they will be My people. I will rejoice over them and be their Shepherd."

Zephaniah rejoiced too. There was sorrow in his heart for those who had shut their ears to his words and soon would be no more, but there was joy that once more, instead of having a lukewarm, deceitful, violent, idol-worshiping nation, God would have a people who would love Him, who would be His own.

Zephaniah must have rejoiced too that he had been able, by walking around the country talking to people, to rescue a whole section of the population from destruction. Of course, *they* did the actual turning to God themselves, but Zephaniah had the satisfaction of knowing that they would not have had the chance to be spared if he had not gone out to speak to them. Few prophets were given such a fearful and yet such a satisfying job.

God had cleaned house in the land of His chosen people. Once more they would truly be His people.

Zephaniah

CHAPTER 1

SUBJECT: A MESSAGE FROM THE LORD.

To: Zephaniah (son of Cushi, grandson of Gedaliah, great-grandson of Amariah, and great-great-grandson of Hezekiah).

When: During the reign of Josiah (son of Amon) king of Judah.[1]

2-6 "I will sweep away everything in all your land," says the Lord. "I will destroy it to the ground. I will sweep away both men and animals alike. Mankind and all the idols that he worships—all will vanish. Even the birds of the air and the fish in the sea will perish. I will crush Judah and Jerusalem with My fist, and destroy every remnant of those who worship Baal; I will put an end to their idolatrous priests, so that even the memory of them will disappear. They go up on their roofs and bow to the sun, moon and stars. They 'follow the Lord,' but worship Molech, too! I will destroy them. And I will destroy those who formerly worshiped the Lord, but now no longer do, and those who never loved Him and never wanted to."

7-9 Stand in silence in the presence of the Lord. For the awesome day of His judgment has come; He has prepared a great slaughter of His people and has chosen their executioners.[2] "On that day of judgment I will punish the leaders and princes of Judah, and all others wearing heathen clothing.[3] Yes, I will punish those who follow heathen customs and who rob and kill to fill their masters' homes with evil gain of violence and fraud.

10-11 A cry of alarm will begin at the farthest gate of Jerusalem, coming closer and closer until the noise of the advancing army reaches the very top of the hill where the city is built. Wail in sorrow, you people of Jerusalem. All your greedy businessmen, all your loan sharks—all will die.

12-13 I will search with lanterns in Jerusalem's darkest

---

[1]Note: The Great Revival under King Josiah followed about 10 years after this prophecy, and then, a dozen years later, the deportation and exile. The prophet Jeremiah was active during this same period.

[2]Literally, "He has prepared a sacrifice and sanctified his guests."

[3]i.e., showing their desire for foreign gods and foreign ways, and their contempt for the Lord.

corners to find and punish those who sit contented in their sins, indifferent to God, thinking He will let them alone. They are the very ones whose property will be plundered by the enemy, whose homes will be ransacked; they will never have a chance to live in the new homes they have built. They will never drink wine from the vineyards they have planted."

14-18 That terrible day is near. Swiftly it comes—a day when strong men will weep bitterly. It is a day of the wrath of God poured out; it is a day of terrible distress and anguish; a day of ruin and desolation; of darkness, gloom, clouds, blackness, trumpet calls and battle cries; down go the walled cities and strongest battlements! "I will make you as helpless as a blind man searching for a path, because you have sinned against the Lord; therefore your blood will be poured out into the dust and your bodies will lie there rotting on the ground." Your silver and gold will be of no use to you in that day of the Lord's wrath. You cannot ransom yourselves with it.[4] For the whole land will be devoured by the fire of His jealousy. He will make a speedy riddance of all the people of Judah.

CHAPTER 2

Gather together and pray, you shameless nation,

2-3 While there still is time—before judgment begins, and your opportunity is blown away like chaff; before the fierce anger of the Lord falls and the terrible day of His wrath begins. Beg Him to save you, all who are humble—all who have tried to obey. Walk humbly and do what is right; perhaps even yet the Lord will protect you from His wrath in that day of doom.

4-5 Gaza, Ashkelon, Ashdod, Ekron—these Philistine cities, too, will be rooted out and left in desolation. And woe to you Philistines[1] living on the coast and in the land of Canaan; for the judgment is against you, too. The Lord will destroy you until not one of you is left.

6-7 The coastland will become a pasture, a place of shepherd camps and folds for sheep. There the little remnant of the tribe of Judah will be pastured. They will lie down to rest in the abandoned houses in Ashkelon. For the Lord God will visit His people in kindness and restore their prosperity again.

[4]Implied.
[1]Literally, "Cherethites (or Cretans)." With the Philistines, they were part of a great wave of immigrants to the southern coast of Palestine around 1200 B.C.

8-10 "I have heard the taunts of the people of Moab and Ammon, mocking My people and invading their land. Therefore as I live," says the Lord of Hosts, God of Israel, "Moab and Ammon will be destroyed like Sodom and Gomorrah, and become a place of stinging nettles and salt pits and eternal desolation; those of My people who are left will plunder and possess them." They will receive the wages of their pride, for they have scoffed at the people of the Lord of Hosts.

11-15 The Lord will do terrible things to them. He will starve out all these gods of foreign powers; and everyone shall worship Him, each in his own land throughout the world. You Ethiopians, too, will be slain by His sword, And so will the lands of the north; He will destroy Assyria and make its great capital Nineveh a desolate wasteland like a wilderness. That once proud city will become a pastureland for sheep. All sorts of wild animals will have their homes in her. Hedgehogs will burrow there; the vultures and the owls will live among the ruins of her palaces, hooting from the gaping windows; the ravens will croak from her doors. All her cedar paneling will lie open to the wind and weather. This is the fate of that vast, prosperous city that lived in such security, that said to herself, "In all the world there is no city as great as I."

But now—see how she has become a place of utter ruins, a place for animals to live! Everyone passing that way will mock, or shake his head in disbelief.[2]

CHAPTER 3

WOE TO FILTHY, SINFUL JERUSALEM, city of violence and crime.

2-4 In her pride she won't listen even to the voice of God. No one can tell her anything; she refuses all correction. She does not trust the Lord, nor seek for God. Her leaders are like roaring lions hunting for their victims—out for everything that they can get. Her judges are like ravenous wolves at evening time, who by dawn have left no trace of their prey. Her "prophets" are liars seeking their own gain; her priests defile the temple by their disobedience to God's laws.

[2]"Nothing then seemed more improbable than that the capital of so vast an empire, a city 60 miles around with walls 100 feet high and so thick that three chariots could go abreast on them, and with 1500 towers, should be so totally destroyed that its site is with difficulty discovered."   —Jamieson, Fausset and Brown Commentary

5-8   But the Lord is there within the city, and He does no wrong. Day by day His justice is more evident, but no one heeds—the wicked know no shame. "I have cut off many nations, laying them waste to their farthest borders; I have left their streets in silent ruin and their cities deserted without a single survivor to remember what happened. I thought, 'Surely they will listen to Me now—surely they will heed My warnings, to that I'll not need to strike again.' But no; however much I punish them, they continue all their evil ways from dawn to dusk and dusk to dawn." But the Lord says, "Be patient; the time is coming soon when I will stand up and accuse these evil nations. For it is My decision to gather together the kingdoms of the earth, and pour out My fiercest anger and wrath upon them. All the earth shall be devoured with the fire of My jealousy.

9-10   "At that time I will change the speech of My returning people to pure Hebrew[1] so that all can worship the Lord together. Those who live far beyond the rivers of Ethiopia will come with their offerings, asking Me to be their God again.

11-13   "And then you will no longer need to be ashamed of yourselves, for you will no longer be rebels against Me. I will remove all your proud and arrogant men from among you; there will be no pride or haughtiness on My holy mountain. Those who are left will be the poor and the humble, and they will trust in the Name of the Lord. They will not be sinners, full of lies and deceit. They will live quietly, in peace, and lie down in safety, and no one will make them afraid."

14-18   Sing, O daughter of Zion; shout, O Israel; be glad and rejoice with all your heart, O daughter of Jerusalem. For the Lord will remove His hand of judgment, and disperse the armies of your enemy. And the Lord Himself, the King of Israel, will live among you! At last your troubles will be over—you need fear no more. On that day the announcement to Jerusalem will be, "Cheer up, don't be afraid. For the Lord your God has arrived to live among you. He is a mighty Saviour. He will give you victory. He will rejoice over you in great gladness; He will love you and not accuse you." Is that a joyous choir I hear? No, it is the Lord Himself exulting over you in happy song: "I have gathered your wounded and taken away your reproach.

19   "And I will deal severely with all who have oppressed you.

[1]Literally, ". . . I will change the speech of the peoples to a pure speech . . ." See Isaiah 19:18.

I will save the weak and helpless ones, and bring together those who were chased away. I will give glory to My former exiles, mocked and shamed.

20 "At that time, I will gather you together and bring you home again, and give you a good name, a name of distinction among all the peoples of the earth; and they will praise you when I restore your fortunes before your very eyes," says the Lord.

Minor Prophets? First,
tell me who the Major Prophets were!

Are You Putting Your Money In A Bag Full Of Holes?

SOMETHING STRANGE WAS GOING ON in the land of Judah.

There wasn't a lot to eat because the crops had failed, but the funny part was that what food they had didn't satisfy anyone's hunger. Though people ate and ate, they still felt hungry.

And it wasn't just food that seemed bewitched. On chilly days, though people piled on more and more clothes, they couldn't get warm. Farmers planted more and more seed in hope of getting at least some sort of a crop, but it made no difference; almost nothing came up anyway. Money was nearly worthless, and no one had enough of it to buy the things they needed.

People had never seen anything like it. There was certainly something strange going on—something weird, something that couldn't be explained.

Then one day Haggai the prophet came to Jerusalem, climbed up on a box in the marketplace, and began speaking to the people:

"Are you eating more lately, but never getting full? Are you buying more and more clothes, yet never have enough to wear? And you who work for wages—does your money slip through your hands so fast that it seems like you're bringing home your pay in a bag full of holes?

"You never have enough of anything, and you can't imagine why?"

His audience was right with him, so Haggai loosened his desert-style headdress a notch and went on:

"I'll give you a hint. Take a look at that building over there."

The people turned to look, although they already knew what they'd see—the temple. Or, more accurately, what *used to be* the temple; it had been reduced to a pile of rubble many years before, and no one had cared enough to build it up again. What had once been a magnificent building now lay in shambles—a confusion of stones littering the ground.

"If you still wonder why things aren't going right for you," Haggai added, "I'll give you a second hint. Think for a moment about what your own homes look like." He knew that most of them were proud of their beautiful homes.

"Is it right that you keep making your homes even more beautiful, and the temple lies in ruins? You keep saying that some day you'll rebuild the house of God, but you never get around to it. How many years has it been since you and your children have had a place in which to worship? Because you have had no temple, you have drifted far from God.

"God has sent blight to shrivel your crops, mildew to rot them, and hail to dash them to pieces, hoping that you would turn to Him for help. But you have not. He has sent drought—the rains ceased and the dew dried up—yet you have gone on ignoring Him. He has sent sickness and death among you and your children, yet you would not call upon Him."

Haggai looked over the audience and was amazed: the people were still listening!

"Now," he proceeded, "God says it *is* time to rebuild His house, time you had a place in which to come into His presence and learn of Him. Therefore, God commands you to go up into the hills and bring wood and build His house."

The people took Haggai's message to heart; they began thinking about how far they had slipped from God—and so did Zerubbabel, the governor of Judah, and Joshua, the high priest, who immediately began drawing up plans for the new temple.

Within a few days men were dispatched into the hills to find wood, and, upon their return, the people began rebuilding the temple. But, as the work proceeded, a grumbling could be heard among the onlookers: "The new temple sure isn't going to be much to look at!" "Couldn't they have planned a more ornate building?" "Such a drab-looking place!"

God spoke again to Haggai. "Tell the governor and the high priest and all the people these words: 'Some of you remember

100

how beautiful the old temple was—a thing of splendor, a thing of glory. In comparison, the new one is nothing. But do not despair; keep working on it, and in a little while I will overthrow many nations and will bring their treasures here to beautify it—their gold and their silver and their precious stones—which are Mine, after all. Then the splendor of this temple will be even greater than that of the former one.

"And tell the people that since the day when they laid the first stone for the foundation of the temple, I have made their fields and their orchards and their vineyards to bring forth abundantly. Now that My people have returned to Me, they will eat and be filled, they will have all the clothing they need, and I will remove the holes from the bags in which they bring home their wages."

Haggai

S*UBJECT:* A MESSAGE FROM THE LORD.

To: Haggai the prophet, who delivered the message to Zerubbabel (son of Shealtiel), Governor of Judah; and to Joshua (son of Josedech), the High Priest—for it was addressed to them.[1]

When: In late August of the second year of the reign of King Darius I.

2-4 "Why is everyone saying it is not the right time for rebuilding My Temple?" asks the Lord His reply to them is this: "Is it then the right time for you to live in luxurious homes, when the Temple lies in ruins?

5-6 Look at the result: You plant much but harvest little. You have scarcely enough to eat or drink, and not enough clothes to keep you warm. Your income disappears, as though you were putting it into pockets filled with holes!"

7-8 "Think it over," says the Lord of Hosts. "Consider how you have acted, and what has happened as a result! Then go up into the mountains and bring down timber, and rebuild My Temple; and I will be pleased with it and appear there in My glory," says the Lord.

9-11 "You hope for much but get so little. And when you bring it home, I blow it away—it doesn't last at all. Why? Because My Temple lies in ruins and you don't care. Your only concern is your own fine homes. That is why I am holding back the rains from heaven and giving you such scant crops. In fact, I have called for a drought upon the land, yes, and in the highlands, too; a drought to wither the grain and grapes and olives and all your other crops; a drought to starve both you and all your cattle, and ruin everything you have worked so hard to get.

12-15 Then Zerubbabel (son of Shealtiel), the governor of Judah, and Joshua (son of Josedech), the High Priest, and the few people remaining in the land obeyed Haggai's message from the Lord their God; they began to worship Him in earnest. Then the Lord told them (again sending the message through Haggai,

[1]Note: They were among the exiles who had returned from Babylon to rebuild Jerusalem.

102

His messenger), "I am with you; I will bless you." And the Lord gave them a desire to rebuild His Temple; so they all gathered in early September of the second year of King Darius' reign, and volunteered their help.

CHAPTER 2

IN EARLY OCTOBER of the same year, the Lord sent them this message through Haggai:

2-6 Ask this question of the governor and high priest and everyone left in the land: "Who among you can remember the Temple as it was before? How glorious it was! In comparison, it is nothing now, is it? But take courage, O Zerubbabel and Joshua and all the people; take courage and work, for 'I am with you,' says the Lord of Hosts. 'For I promised when you left Egypt that My Spirit would remain among you; so don't be afraid. For the Lord of Hosts says, 'In just a little while I will begin to shake the heavens and earth—and the oceans, too, and the dry land—

7-9 "I will shake all nations; and the Desire of All Nations[1] shall come to this Temple; and I will fill this place with My glory,' says the Lord of Hosts. 'The future splendor of this Temple will be greater than the splendor of the first one! For I have plenty of silver and gold to do it! And here I will give peace,'[2] says the Lord."

10-13 In early December, in the second year of the reign of King Darius, this message came from the Lord through Haggai the prophet: Ask the priests this question about the law: "If one of you is carrying a holy sacrifice in his robes, and happens to brush against some bread or wine or meat, will it too become holy?" "No," the priests replied. "Holiness does not pass to other things that way." Then Haggai asked, "But if someone touches a dead person, and so becomes ceremonially impure, and then brushes against something, does it become contaminated?"

And the priests answered, "Yes."

14-15 Haggai then made his meaning clear. "You people," he said (speaking for the Lord), "were contaminating your sacrifices by living with selfish attitudes and evil hearts—and not only your sacrifices, but everything else that you did as a 'service' to

[1] i.e., Christ, the Messiah. Literally, "The Treasures" or "that which is choice." But many commentators prefer this rendering: "The treasures of the nations will pour into this temple, and I will fill it with splendor."

[2] Peace with God through Christ Who, 500 years later, came often to this temple.

103

me. And so everything you did went wrong. But all is different now, because you have begun to build the Temple.

16-19 "Before, when you expected a twenty bushel crop, there were only ten. When you came to draw fifty gallons from the olive press, there were only twenty. I rewarded all your labor with rust and mildew and hail. Yet, even so, you refused to return to Me," says the Lord. "But now note this: From today, this 24th day of the month,[3] as the foundation of the Lord's Temple is finished, and from this day onward, I will bless you. Notice, I am giving you this promise now before you have even begun to rebuild the temple structure, and before you have harvested your grain, and before the grapes and figs and pomegranates and olives have produced their next crops: *from this day I will bless you.*"

20 Another message came to Haggai from the Lord that same day:

21-23 Tell Zerubbabel, the Governor of Judah, "I am about to shake the heavens and the earth, And to overthrow thrones and destroy the strength of the kingdoms of the nations. I will overthrow their armed might, and brothers and companions will kill each other. But when that happens, I will take you, O Zerubbabel My servant, and honor you like a signet ring upon My finger; for I have specially chosen you," says the Lord of Hosts.

[3]"The 24th day of Kislev." This corresponds to early in our December.

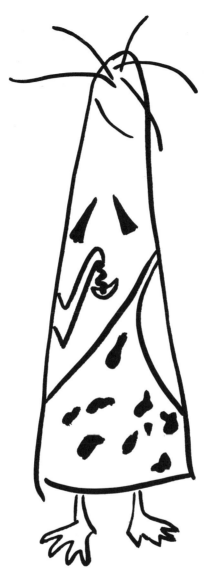

*The prophets lived in the wilderness
and hung skins over their bony shoulders and
ate grasshoppers. That's real dedication!*

My Dreams
Are Getting Weirder
All The Time

IF YOU THINK *you've* been having crazy nightmares lately, consider the weird assortment of things that Zechariah the prophet had disturbing his sleep: two women, flapping their stork-like wings, lugging a lead-lidded crock with a third woman inside it back and forth, back and forth, between heaven and earth; Joshua the priest wandering around in dirty old clothes; four chariots, one pulled by red horses, one by black, one by white, and one by dappled gray, dashing out from between two mountains of bronze.

Mix in a flying scroll, a man with a measuring line, four horns of some sort, Satan, and an accumulation of gold lamps, bowls, and pipes, and you have enough to cause even the most stout-hearted sleeper to prefer insomnia, or to make Freud give up in confusion.

Luckily, Zechariah had an interpreter; standing nearby, temporarily unemployed, was an angel of the more knowledgeable sort.

"Look," said the angel, taking Zechariah figuratively by the hand, "I will explain this hallucination-type horror to you. To start with, this bunch of people you live among is, shall we say, not on the best terms with God. Ignoring his commands and all that. Pretty rotten. Foul, even. God has watched the goings-on long enough. He is angry. And jealous. He is tired of punishing, tired of giving the back of His hand. So now He makes a new offer: return to Him, and He will return to you."

Zechariah weighed and considered the proposal. Reasonable

106

enough it was. And more: it was a word from God. And so he told the people.

The people listened and realized that they had slipped away from God, and many began to walk in His ways again.

A few weeks later there came a knocking at Zechariah's door, a deputation from the town of Bethel.

"We're wondering," the spokesman began, "which of our old practices we should keep now that we've begun worshiping God again. Particularly we're wondering about this business of fasting. All during the 70 years that we were in exile in Babylon, we fasted and mourned during the fifth and seventh months. Should we keep on doing this?"

More rapid than eagles, God's answer came through Zechariah: "While you were in captivity those 70 years, was it actually for God that you fasted? And when you eat and drink now, do you not do it for yourselves?"

The deputation listened intently.

"So—God says for you to turn your fast months into feast months. Instead of fasting, show kindness and mercy to each other. Stop oppressing the widow, the fatherless, the visitor, and the poor. Love truth and peace."

"But—" wailed the spokesman for Bethel, "look at how bad the times are!" He wrung his hands symbolically. "Maybe fasting would help!"

"Forget the fasting," Zechariah ordered emphatically, "and turn to God. If you want conditions to be different, be different men. Begin practicing justice and brotherhood. Try to understand those around you. Be tolerant of those who are different from you. Speak the truth with each other. Fasting is a small matter; if you have truly turned to God, show it in the way you treat each other."

The deputation from Bethel lingered for a few minutes to let Zechariah's words sink in, then set off.

Somehow it was not easy to think of giving up fasting. It had so much to recommend it—the feeling of righteousness that pervaded one's soul after one had gone a whole day without food, the sense of superiority over one's non-fasting brother, the smug assurance that one had obeyed the law to the letter.

But Zechariah had not finished prophesying; he still had a message from God about the coming of the Savior:

107

"The people wander like sheep;
  they are afflicted for want of a shepherd.
Behold, I will bring my servant the Branch.
Lo, your king comes to you;
  triumphant and victorious is He,
humble and riding on an ass,
  on a colt the foal of an ass.
When they look on Him whom they have pierced,
  they shall mourn for Him.
And He shall command peace to the nations;
  His dominion shall be from sea to sea,
    and from the River to the ends of the earth."

Zechariah

*S*UBJECT: MESSAGES FROM THE LORD.

These messages from the Lord were given to Zechariah (son of Berechiah, and grandson of Iddo the prophet) in early November of the second year of the reign of King Darius.

* * * *

2-6 The Lord of Hosts was very angry with your fathers. But He will turn again and favor you if only you return to Him. Don't be like your fathers were! The earlier prophets pled in vain with them to turn from all their evil ways. "Come, return to Me," the Lord God said, but no, they wouldn't listen; they paid no attention at all. Your fathers and their prophets are now long dead, but remember the lesson they learned, that *God's word endures!* It caught up with them and punished them. Then at last they repented. "We have gotten what we deserved from God," they said, "He has done just what He warned us He would."

* * * *

7 The following February, still in the second year of the reign of King Darius, another message from the Lord came to Zechariah (son of Berechiah and grandson of Iddo the prophet), in a vision in the night:

8-9 I saw a man sitting on a red horse that was standing among the myrtle trees beside a river. Behind him were other horses, red and bay and white, each with its rider.[1] An angel stood beside me, and I asked him, "Sir, what are all those horses for?"

"I'll tell you," he replied.

10 Then the rider on the red horse—he was the Angel of the Lord—answered me, "The Lord has sent them to patrol the earth for Him."

11 Then the other riders reported to the Angel of the Lord, "We have patrolled the whole earth, and everywhere there is prosperity and peace."

[1]Implied.

109

12   Upon hearing this, the Angel of the Lord prayed this prayer: "O Lord of Hosts, for seventy years Your anger has raged against Jerusalem and the cities of Judah. How long will it be until You again show mercy to them?"

13   And the Lord answered the angel who stood beside me, speaking words of comfort and assurance.

14-17   Then the angel said, "Shout out this message from the Lord of Hosts: Don't you think I care about what has happened to Judah and Jerusalem? I am as jealous as a husband for his captive wife. I am very angry with the heathen nations sitting around at ease; for I was only a little displeased with My people, but the nations afflicted them far beyond My intentions. Therefore the Lord declares: I have returned to Jerusalem filled with mercy; My Temple will be rebuilt, says the Lord of Hosts and so will all Jerusalem. Say it again: the Lord of Hosts declares that the cities of Israel will again overflow with prosperity, and the Lord will again comfort Jerusalem and bless her and live in her."

18-19   Then I looked and saw four animal horns! "What are these?" I asked the angel.

He replied, "They represent the four world powers that have scattered Judah, Israel and Jerusalem."

20-21   Then the Lord showed me four blacksmiths. "What have these men come to do?" I asked. The angel replied, "They have come to take hold of the four horns that scattered Judah so terribly, and to pound them on the anvil and throw them away."

CHAPTER 2

WHEN I LOOKED AROUND ME AGAIN, I saw a man carrying a yardstick in his hand.

2   "Where are you going?" I asked.

"To measure Jerusalem," he said; "I want to see whether it is big enough for all the people!"

3-5   Then the angel who was talking to me went over to meet another angel coming towards him. "Go tell this young man," said the other angel, "that Jerusalem will someday be so full of people that she won't have room enough for all! Many will live outside the city walls, with all their many cattle—and yet they will be safe. For the Lord Himself will be a wall of fire protecting them and all Jerusalem; He will be the glory of the city.

6-9   " 'Come, flee from the land of the north, from Babylon,' says the Lord to all His exiles there; 'I scattered you to the winds but I will bring you back again. Escape, escape to Zion now!' says the Lord. The Lord of Glory has sent Me[1] against the nations that oppressed you, for he who harms you sticks his finger in Jehovah's eye! 'I will smash them with My fist and their slaves will be their rulers! *Then you will know it was the Lord of Hosts who sent Me.*

10-12 "Sing, Jerusalem, and rejoice! For I have come to live among you,' says the Lord. 'At that time many nations will be converted to the Lord, and they too shall be My people; I will live among them all. *Then you will know it was the Lord of Hosts who sent Me to you.* And Judah shall be the Lord's inheritance in the Holy Land, for God shall once more choose to bless Jerusalem.'

13 "Be silent, all mankind, before the Lord; for He has come to earth from heaven, from His holy home."

CHAPTER 3

THEN THE ANGEL SHOWED ME (in my vision) Joshua the High Priest standing before the Angel of the Lord; and Satan was there too, at the Angel's right hand, accusing Joshua of many things.

2 But the Lord said to Satan, "I reject your accusations,* Satan; yes, I, the Lord, for I have decided to be merciful to Jerusalem—I rebuke you. I have decreed mercy to Joshua and his nation; they are like a burning stick pulled out of the fire."

3-4 Joshua's clothing was filthy as he stood before the Angel of the Lord. Then the Angel said to the others standing there, "Remove his filthy clothing." And turning to Joshua He said, "See, I have taken away your sins; and now I am giving you these fine new clothes."

5-10 Then I said, "Please, could he also have a clean turban on his head?" So they gave him one. Then the Angel of the Lord spoke very solemnly to Joshua and said, "The Lord of Hosts declares: 'If you will follow the paths I set for you and do all I tell you to, then I will put you in charge of My temple, to keep it holy; and I will let you walk in and out of My presence with these angels. Listen to Me, O Joshua the high priest, and all you

[1]This passage evidently refers to the Messiah, here seen as one of the Godhead.
*Literally, "The Lord rebuke you, O Satan; even the Lord, who has chosen Jerusalem, rebuke you. Is not this a brand plucked out of the fire?"

111

other priests, you are illustrations of the good things to come. Don't you see?—Joshua represents My Servant The Branch* whom I will send. He will be the Foundation Stone of the temple that Joshua is standing beside, and I will engrave this inscription on it seven times.‡ *I will remove the sins of this land in a single day.* And after that,' the Lord of Hosts declares, 'you will all live in peace and prosperity and each of you will own a home of your own where you can invite your neighbors.' "

CHAPTER 4

THEN THE ANGEL who had been talking with me woke me, as though I had been asleep.

2-3 "What do you see now?" he asked. I answered, "I see a golden lampstand holding seven lamps, and at the top there is a reservoir for the olive oil that feeds the lamps, flowing into them through seven tubes. And I see two olive trees carved upon the lampstand, one on each side of the reservoir.

4 "What is it, sir?" I asked. "What does this mean?"

5 "Don't you really know?" the angel asked.

"No, sir," I said, "I don't."

6-8 Then he said, "This is God's message to Zerubbabel;[1] 'Not by might, nor by power, but by My Spirit, says the Lord of Hosts—you will succeed because of My Spirit, though you are few and weak.' Therefore no mountain, however high, can stand before Zerubbabel! For it will flatten out before him! And Zerubbabel will finish building this temple[2] with mighty shouts of thanksgiving for God's mercy, declaring that all was done by grace alone."[3]

Another message that I received from the Lord said:

9-10 "Zerubbabel laid the foundation of this temple, and he will complete it. (Then you will know these messages are from God, the Lord of Hosts.) Do not despise this small beginning, for the eyes of the Lord rejoice to see the work begin, to see the plumbline in the hand of Zerubbabel. For these seven lamps represent the eyes of the Lord that see around the world."

*i.e., the Messiah, Christ.
‡Literally, "See the stone with seven facets I have set before Joshua; and I will engrave its inscription."
[1]Governor of Judah, who was given the responsibility for rebuilding the temple. See Haggai 1:1; 2:23, etc.
[2]Literally, "He will bring forth the capstone."
[3]Or, "with mighty shouts, 'How beautiful it is,' " or, "the Lord bless it!"

11-12 Then I asked him about the two olive trees on each side of the lampstand, and about the two olive branches that emptied oil into golden bowls through two golden tubes.

13 "Don't you know?" he asked. "No, sir," I said.

14 Then he told me, "They represent the two anointed ones who assist the Lord of all the earth."

CHAPTER 5

I LOOKED UP AGAIN and saw a scroll flying through the air.

2 "What do you see?" he asked. "A flying scroll!" I replied. "It appears to be about thirty feet long and fifteen feet wide!"

3-4 "This scroll," he told me, "represents the words of God's curse going out over the entire land. It says that all who steal and lie have been judged and sentenced to death.

"I am sending this curse into the home of every thief and everyone who swears falsely by My Name," says the Lord of Hosts. "And My curse shall remain upon his home and completely destroy it."

5 Then the angel left me for awhile, but he returned and said, "Look up! Something is traveling through the sky!"

6 "What is it?" I asked.

He replied, "It is a bushel basket filled with the sin prevailing everywhere throughout the land."

7-9 Suddenly the heavy lead cover on the basket was lifted off, and I could see a woman sitting inside the basket! He said, "She represents wickedness," and he pushed her back into the basket and clamped down the heavy lid again. Then I saw two women flying toward us, with wings like those of a stork. And they took the bushel basket and flew off with it, high in the sky.

10 "Where are they taking her?" I asked the angel.

11 He replied, "To Babylon[1] where she belongs and where she will stay!"

CHAPTER 6

THEN I LOOKED UP AGAIN and saw four chariots coming from between what looked like two mountains made of brass.

2-3 The first chariot was pulled by red horses, the second by

[1]Babylon had, by the time of Zechariah, become a symbol, the center of world idolatry and wickedness.

black ones, The third by white horses and the fourth by dappled-greys.

4 "And what are these, sir?" I asked the angel.

5-6 He replied, "These are the four heavenly spirits who stand before the Lord of all the earth; they are going out to do His work. The chariot pulled by the black horses will go north, and the one pulled by white horses will follow it there,[1] while the dappled-greys will go south."

7 The red[2] horses were impatient to be off, to patrol back and forth across the earth, so the Lord said, "Go. Begin your patrol." So they left at once.

8-9 Then the Lord summoned me and said, "Those who went north have executed My judgment and quieted My anger there." In another message the Lord said:

10-11 "Heldai, Tobijah and Jedaiah will bring gifts of silver and gold from the Jews exiled in Babylon. The same day they arrive, meet them at the home of Josiah (son of Zephaniah), where they will stay. Accept their gifts and make from them a crown from the silver and gold. Then put the crown on the head of Joshua (son of Josedech) the high priest.

12-13 Tell him that the Lord of Hosts says, 'You represent the Man who will come, whose name is The Branch—He will grow up from Himself[3]—and will build the Temple of the Lord. To Him belongs the royal title. He will rule both as King and as Priest, with perfect harmony between the two!'

14-15 Then put the crown in the temple of the Lord, to honor those who gave it—Heldai, Tobijah, Jedaiah, and also Josiah. These three who have come from so far away represent many others who will some day come from distant lands to rebuild the Temple of the Lord. And when this happens you will know my messages have been from God, the Lord of Hosts. But none of this will happen unless you carefully obey the commandments of the Lord your God."

CHAPTER 7

ANOTHER MESSAGE CAME TO ME from the Lord in late November of the fourth year of the reign of King Darius.

2-3 The Jews of the city of Bethel had sent a group of men

[1]Or, "will go west."
[2]"Red" implied.
[3]Literally, "He will grow up in His place."

headed by Sharezer, the chief administrative officer of the king, and Regemmelech, to the Lord's temple at Jerusalem, to seek His blessing, and to speak with the priests and prophets about whether they must continue their traditional custom of fasting and mourning during the month of August each year, as they had been doing so long.

4-7   This was the Lord's reply: "When you return to Bethel, say to all your people and your priests, 'During those seventy years of exile when you fasted and mourned in August and October, were you really in earnest about leaving your sins behind, and coming back to Me? No, not at all! And even now in your holy feasts to God, you don't think of Me, but only of the food and fellowship and fun. Long years ago, when Jerusalem was prosperous and her southern suburbs out along the plain were filled with people, the prophets warned them that this attitude would surely lead to ruin, as it has.' "

*   *   *   *

8-10   Then this message from the Lord came to Zechariah. "Tell them to be honest and fair—and not to take bribes—and to be merciful and kind to everyone. Tell them to stop oppressing widows and orphans, foreigners and poor people; and to stop plotting evil against each other.

11-12   Your fathers would not listen to this message. They turned stubbornly away and put their fingers in their ears to keep from hearing Me. They hardened their hearts like flint, afraid to hear the words that God, the Lord of Hosts, commanded them—the laws He had revealed to them by His Spirit through the early prophets. That is why such great wrath came down on them from God.

13-14   I called but they refused to listen; so when they cried to Me, I turned away. I scattered them as with a whirlwind among the far-off nations. Their land became desolate; no one even traveled through it; the Pleasant Land lay bare and blighted."

CHAPTER 8

AGAIN THE LORD'S MESSAGE CAME TO ME:

2-4   "The Lord of Hosts says, I am greatly concerned—yes, furiously angry—because of all that Jerusalem's enemies have done to her. Now I am going to return to My land and I, Myself, will live within Jerusalem; and Jerusalem shall be called 'The

Faithful City,' and 'The Holy Mountain,' and 'The Mountain of the Lord of Hosts.' " The Lord of Hosts declares that Jerusalem will have peace and prosperity so long that there will once again be aged men and women hobbling through her streets on canes;

5-8 "And the streets will be filled with boys and girls at play. The Lord says, "This seems unbelievable to you—a remnant, small, discouraged as you are—but it is no great thing for Me. You can be sure that I will rescue My people from east and west, wherever they are scattered. I will bring them home again to live safely in Jerusalem; and they will be My people, and I will be their God, just and true and yet forgiving them their sins[1]!"

9-12 The Lord of Hosts says, "Get on with the job and finish it! You have been listening long enough! For since you began laying the foundation of the temple, the prophets have been telling you about the blessings that await you when it's finished. Before the work began there were no jobs, no wages, no security; if you left the city, there was no assurance you would ever return, for crime was rampant. But it is all so different now!" says the Lord of Hosts. "For I am sowing peace and prosperity among you. Your crops will prosper; the grapevines will be weighted down with fruit; the ground will be fertile, with plenty of rain; all these blessings will be given to the people left in the land.

13-15 " 'May you be as poor as Judah,' the heathen used to say to those they cursed! But no longer! For now 'Judah' is a word of blessing, not a curse. 'May you be as prosperous and happy as Judah is,' they'll say. So don't be afraid or discouraged! Get on with rebuilding the temple! If you do, I will certainly bless you. And don't think that I might change My mind. I did what I said I would when your fathers angered Me and I promised to punish them; and I won't change this decision of Mine to bless you.

16-17 "Here is your part: Tell the truth. Be fair. Live at peace with everyone. Don't plot harm to others; don't swear that something is true when it isn't! How I hate all that sort of thing!" says the Lord.

*　　*　　*　　*

18 Here is another message that came to me from the Lord of Hosts:

19-22 "The traditional fasts and times of mourning you have kept in July, August, October, and January[2] are ended. They

[1]Literally, "I will be their God in truth and in righteousness."
[2]Literally, "fourth, fifth, seventh, and tenth months."

116

will be changed to joyous festivals if you love truth and peace! People from around the world will come on pilgrimages and pour into Jerusalem from many foreign cities to attend these celebrations. People will write their friends in other cities and say, 'Let's go to Jerusalem to ask the Lord to bless us, and be merciful to us. I'm going! Please come with me. Let's go *now!*' Yes, many people, even strong nations, will come to the Lord of Hosts in Jerusalem to ask for His blessing and help.

23 "In those days ten men from ten different nations will clutch at the coat sleeves of one Jew and say, 'Please be my friend, for I know that God is with you.' "

CHAPTER 9

THIS IS THE MESSAGE concerning God's curse on the lands of Hadrach and Damascus; for the Lord is closely watching all mankind,[1] as well as Israel:

2-7 "Doomed is Hamath, near Damascus, and Tyre, and Zidon, too, shrewd though they be. Though Tyre has armed herself to the hilt, and become so rich that silver is like dirt to her, and fine gold like dust in the streets, Yet the Lord will dispossess her, and hurl her fortifications into the sea; and she shall be set on fire and burned to the ground. Ashkelon will see it happen and be filled with fear; Gaza will huddle in desperation and Ekron will shake with terror, for their hopes that Tyre would stop the enemies' advance will all be dashed. Gaza will be conquered, her king killed; and Ashkelon will be completely destroyed. Foreigners will take over the city of Ashdod, the rich city of the Philistines. I will yank her idolatry out of her mouth, and pull from her teeth her sacrifices that she eats with blood. Everyone left will worship God and be adopted into Israel as a new clan: the Philistines of Ekron will intermarry with the Jews, just as the Jebusites did so long ago.

8-9 "And I will surround My Temple like a guard to keep invading armies from entering Israel. I am closely watching their movements and I will keep them away; no foreign oppressors will again overrun My people's land. Rejoice greatly, O My people! Shout with joy! For look—your King is coming! He is the Righteous One, the Victor! yet He is lowly, riding on a donkey's colt!

[1]Or, "for the cities of Syria belong to the Lord, as much as to the tribes of Israel."

10-11 "I will disarm all peoples of the earth, including My people in Israel, and He shall bring peace among the nations. His realm shall stretch from sea to sea, from the river to the ends of the earth.[2] I have delivered you from death in a waterless pit, because of the covenant I made with you, sealed with blood.

12-15 "Come to the place of safety, all you prisoners; for there is yet hope! I promise right now, I will repay you two mercies for each of your woes! Judah, you are My bow! Ephraim, you are My arrow! Both of you will be My sword like the sword of a mighty soldier brandished against the sons of Greece." The Lord shall lead His people as they fight! His arrows shall fly like lightning; the Lord God shall sound the trumpet call and go out against His enemies like a whirlwind off the desert from the south. He will defend His people and they will subdue their enemies, treading them beneath their feet. They will taste victory and shout with triumph. They will slaughter their foes, leaving horrible carnage everywhere.

16-17 The Lord their God will save His people in that day, as a Shepherd caring for His sheep. They shall shine in His land as glittering jewels in a crown. How wonderful and beautiful all shall be! The abundance of grain and wine will make the young men and girls flourish; they will be radiant with health and happiness.

CHAPTER 10

ASK THE LORD FOR RAIN in the springtime, and He will answer with lightning and showers. Every field will become a lush pasture.

2 How foolish to ask the idols for anything like that! Fortune-tellers' predictions are all a bunch of silly lies; what comfort is there in promises that don't come true? Judah and Israel have been led astray and wander like lost sheep; everyone attacks them, for they have no shepherd to protect them.

3-5 "My anger burns against your 'shepherds'—your leaders —and I will punish them—these goats. For the Lord of Hosts has arrived to help His flock of Judah. I will make them strong and glorious like a proud steed in battle. From them will come the Cornerstone, the Peg on which all hope hangs, the Bow that wins

[2]Or, "to the ends of the land" of Palestine. Either interpretation is possible from the Hebrew text, but many other passages indicate Christ's universal rule.

118

the battle, the Ruler over all the earth.[1] They will be mighty warriors for God, grinding their enemies' faces into the dust beneath their feet. The Lord is with them as they fight; their enemy is doomed.

6-7 "I will strengthen Judah, yes, and Israel too; I will re-establish them because I love them. It will be as though I had never cast them all away, for I, the Lord their God, will hear their cries. They shall be like mighty warriors. They shall be happy as with wine. Their children, too, shall see the mercies of the Lord and be glad. Their hearts shall rejoice in the Lord.

8-11 "When I whistle to them, they'll come running, for I have bought them back again. From the few that are left, their population will grow again to former size. Though I have scattered them like seeds among the nations, still they will remember Me and return again to God; with all their children, they will come home again to Israel. I will bring them back from Egypt and Assyria, and resettle them in Israel—in Gilead and Lebanon; there will scarcely be room for all of them! They shall pass safely through the sea of distress,[2] for the waves will be held back. The Nile will become dry—the rule of Assyria and Egypt over My people will end."

12 The Lord says, "I will make My people strong with power frcm Me! They will go wherever they wish; and wherever they go, they will be under My personal care."

CHAPTER 11

OPEN YOUR DOORS, O Lebanon, to judgment.[1] You will be destroyed as though by fire raging through your forests.

2 Weep, O cypress trees, for all the ruined cedars; the tallest and most beautiful of them are fallen. Cry in fear, you oaks of Bashan, as you watch the thickest forests felled.

3 Listen to the wailing of Israel's leaders—all these evil shepherds—for their wealth is gone. Hear the young lions roaring—the princes are weeping, for their glorious Jordan valley lies in ruins.

* * * *

4-6 Then said the Lord my God to me, "Go and take a job as

[1] i.e., The Messiah.
[2] Or, "the Sea of Egypt," referring to the Red Sea which the people of Israel were miraculously brought through when God brought them out of slavery the first time.
[1] Implied.

shepherd of a flock being fattened for the butcher. This will illustrate the way My people have been bought and slain by wicked leaders, who go unpunished. 'Thank God, now I am rich!' say those who have betrayed them—their own shepherds have sold them without mercy. And I won't spare them either," says the Lord, "for I will let them fall into the clutches of their own wicked leaders, and they will slay them. They shall turn the land into a wilderness and I will not protect it from them."

7-9 So I took two shepherd's staffs, naming one "Grace" and the other "Union," and I fed the flock as I had been told to do. And I got rid of their three evil shepherds in a single month. But I became impatient with these sheep—this nation—and they hated me too. So I told them, "I won't be your shepherd any longer. If you die, you die; if you are killed, I don't care. Go ahead and destroy yourselves!"

10 And I took my staff called "Grace" and snapped it in two, showing that I had broken my contract to lead and protect them.

11 That was the end of the agreement. Then those who bought and sold sheep, who were watching, realized that God was telling them something through what I did.

12-13 And I said to their leaders, "If you like, give me my pay, whatever I am worth; but only if you want to." So they counted out thirty little silver coins[2] as my wages. And the Lord told me, "Toss it into the temple treasury[3]—this magnificent sum they value you at!" So I took the thirty coins and threw them in.

14 Then I broke my other staff, "Union," to show that the bond of unity between Judah and Israel was broken.

15-17 Then the Lord told me to go again and get a job as a shepherd: this time I was to act the part of a worthless, wicked shepherd. And He said to me, "This illustrates how I will give this nation a shepherd who will not care for the dying ones, nor look after the young, nor heal the broken bones, nor feed the healthy ones, nor carry the lame that cannot walk; instead, he will eat the fat ones, even tearing off their feet. Woe to this worthless shepherd who doesn't care for the flock. God's sword will cut his arm and pierce through his right eye; his arm will become useless and his right eye blinded."

[2]The price of a slave. See Exodus 21:32; and Matthew 27:3-9.
[3]The translation here follows the Syriac version. "Cast it to the potter" is the Hebrew.

THIS IS THE FATE OF ISRAEL, as pronounced by the Lord, who stretched out the heavens and laid the foundation of the earth, and formed the spirit of man within him:

2-5 "I will make Jerusalem and Judah like a cup of poison to all the nearby nations that send their armies to surround Jerusalem. Jerusalem will be a heavy stone burdening the world. And though all the nations of the earth unite to an attempt to move her, they will all be crushed. In that day," says the Lord, "I will bewilder the armies drawn up against her, and make fools of them; for I will watch over the people of Judah, but blind all her enemies. And the clans of Judah shall say to themselves, 'The people of Jerusalem have found strength in the Lord of Hosts, their God.'

6-7 "In that day I will make the clans of Judah like a little fire that sets the forest aflame—like a burning match among the sheaves; they will burn up all the neighboring nations right and left, while Jerusalem stands unmoved. The Lord will give victory to the remainder of Judah first, before Jerusalem; so that the people of Jerusalem and the royal line of David won't be filled with pride at their success.

8-10 "The Lord will defend the people of Jerusalem; the weakest among them will be as mighty as King David! And the royal line will be as God, like the Angel of the Lord who goes before them! For My plan is to destroy all the nations that come against Jerusalem. Then I will pour out the spirit of grace and prayer on all the people of Jerusalem; and they will look on Him they pierced, and mourn for Him as for an only son, and grieve bitterly for Him as for an oldest child who died.

11-14 "The sorrow and mourning in Jerusalem at that time will be even greater than the grievous mourning for the godly king Josiah,[1] who was killed in the valley of Megiddo. All of Israel will weep in profound sorrow. The whole nation will be bowed down with universal grief—king, prophet, priest, and people. Each family will go into private mourning, husband and wives apart, to face their sorrow alone."

CHAPTER 13

AT THAT TIME a Fountain will be opened to the people of

[1]Implied from II Chronicles 35:24, 25. Literally, "Like the mourning of Hadad-rimmon in the valley of Megiddo."

Israel and Jerusalem, a Fountain to cleanse them from all their sins and uncleanness."

2-3 And the Lord of Hosts declares, "In that day I will get rid of every vestige of idol worship throughout the land, so that even the names of the idols will be forgotten. All false prophets and fortune-tellers will be wiped out, and if anyone begins false prophecy again, his own father and mother will slay him! 'You must die,' they will tell him, 'for you are prophesying lies in the name of the Lord.'

4-6 "No one will be boasting then of his prophetic gift! No one will wear prophet's clothes to try to fool the people then. 'No,' he will say. 'I am not a prophet; I am a farmer. The soil has been my livelihood from my earliest youth.' And if someone asks, 'Then what are these scars on your chest and your back?'[1] he will say, 'I got into a brawl at the home of a friend!'[2]

7 "Awake, O sword, against My Shepherd, the man who is my associate and equal," says the Lord of Hosts. "Strike down the Shepherd and the sheep will scatter; but I will come back and comfort and care for the lambs.

8-9 "Two-thirds of all the nation of Israel will be cut off and die,[3] but a third will be left in the land. I will bring the third that remain through the fire and make them pure, as gold and silver are refined and purified by fire. They will call upon My Name and I will hear them; I will say, 'These are My people,' and they will say, 'The Lord is our God.' "

CHAPTER 14

Watch, FOR THE DAY OF THE LORD IS COMING SOON! On that day the Lord will gather together the nations to fight Jerusalem; and the city will be taken, the houses rifled, the loot divided, the women raped; half the population will be taken away as slaves, and half will be left in what remains of the city.

3 Then the Lord will go out fully armed for war, to fight against those nations.

4-5 That day His feet will stand upon the Mount of Olives, to the east of Jerusalem; and the Mount of Olives will split

[1]Evidently self-inflicted cuts, as practiced by false prophets. See I Kings 18:28.

[2]Literally, "(These are) wounds I received in the house of my friends." That this is not a passage referring to Christ, is clear from the context. This is a false prophet who is lying about the reason for his scars.

[3]This has already happened twice: two million Jews perished in the Roman wars, six million under Hitler. Is a yet future disaster foretold here?

apart, making a very wide valley running from east to west; for half the mountain will move toward the north and half toward the south. You will escape through that valley, for it will reach across to the city gate.[1] Yes, you will escape as your people did long centuries ago from the earthquake in the days of Uzziah, king of Judah; and the Lord my God shall come, and all His saints and angels[2] with Him.

6-8 The sun and moon and stars will no longer shine,[3] yet there will be continuous day! Only the Lord knows how! There will be no normal day and night—at evening time it will still be light. Life-giving waters will flow out from Jerusalem, half towards the Dead Sea and half towards the Mediterranean, flowing continuously both in winter and in summer.

9 And the Lord shall be King over all the earth. In that day there shall be one Lord—His name alone will be worshiped.

10-11 All the land from Geba (the northern border of Judah) to Rimmon (the southern border) will become one vast plain, but Jerusalem will be on an elevated site, covering the area all the way from the Gate of Benjamin over to the site of the old gate, then to the Corner Gate, and from the Tower of Hananeel to the king's wine presses. And Jerusalem shall be inhabited, safe at last, never again to be cursed and destroyed.

12-15 And the Lord will send a plague on all the people who fought Jerusalem. They will become like walking corpses, their flesh rotting away; their eyes will shrivel in their sockets, and their tongues will decay in their mouths. They will be seized with terror, panic-stricken from the Lord, and will fight against each other in hand-to-hand combat. All Judah will be fighting at[4] Jerusalem. The wealth of all the neighboring nations will be confiscated—great quantities of gold and silver and fine clothing. (This same plague will strike the horses, mules, camels, donkeys, and all the other animals in the enemy camp.)

16-19 In the end, those who survive the plague will go up to Jerusalem each year to worship the King, the Lord of Hosts; to celebrate a time[5] of thanksgiving. And any nation anywhere in all the world that refuses to come to Jerusalem to worship the

[1]Literally, "for the valley of My mountain shall touch Azel"—apparently a hamlet on the eastern outskirts of Jerusalem.
[2]Literally, "His holy ones."
[3]The Hebrew is uncertain.
[4]Or, "against Jerusalem."
[5]Literally, "the Feast of Tabernacles" or "Booths."

King, the Lord of Hosts, will have no rain. But if Egypt refuses to come, God will punish her with some other plague. And so Egypt and the other nations will all be punished if they refuse to come.

20-21   In that day the bells on the horses will have written on them, "These are Holy Property";[6] and the trash cans in the Temple of the Lord will be as sacred as the bowls beside the altar. In fact, every container in Jerusalem and Judah shall be sacred to the Lord of Hosts; all who come to worship may use any of them free of charge to boil their sacrifices in; there will be no more grasping traders in the temple of the Lord of Hosts!

[6]Literally, "Holy to the Lord."

Major League, Minor League—
Major Prophets, Minor Prophets. They're
both fast leagues for rookies

Shut The Church Doors!

"I WISH THAT THERE WERE SOMEONE among you who would shut the doors of the church and put an end to this farce! Your worship is utter mockery!"

Malachi stood outside the temple and lashed the people with the fury of his words.

"Look at the gifts you bring to God's holy altar!"

"The people glanced sheepishly down at the sacrifices they had brought—sickly lambs, corn full of worms, moldy bread.

"Where is your tithe? Have you forgotten that a tenth belongs to your Maker? Will a man rob God? You have!

"And your priests—they don't teach God's ways. They say, 'What a weariness it is to serve God,' and they sniff at Him."

Malachi did not spare the people. Their sins were many, and he proceeded to recount every one of them.

"Look what you have done with marriage, that holy estate which God created to bless you! Intermarrying with the heathen! Divorce! Violence of every sort!

"And where has your faith dwindled to? You have become so skeptical of God that you say, 'What is the use of living God's way when those who do evil prosper more than we do?' Do you refuse to believe unless you see God's judgment meted out daily upon the disobedient?" Malachi's eyes burned holes in his hearers.

"Do you not know that He loves you, his chosen people? On the Last Day you will see whether or not it pays to have faith in Him. On that day He will be swift against adulterers, against those who speak falsely, against those who oppress their fellow man, against those who have no respect for Him."

Thus spoke God through His prophet Malachi, who some have

126

compared with the wise teacher Socrates. Seven times in this short book Malachi, in a Socratic manner, (1) states a truth, (2) presents the objections that the people raise to that truth, and then (3) gives God's answer to the whole matter.

For instance, this appears in chapter 1, verses 6 and 7:

(1) God says, "A son honors his father, a servant honors his master. I am your Father and Master, yet you don't honor Me, O priests, but you despise My name."

(2) "Who? Us?" you say. "When did we ever despise Your Name?"

(3) God answers: "Every time you say, 'Don't bother bringing anything very valuable to God!'"

But, important as the matters of sacrifice and tithes were to Malachi, he was more concerned about the inward poverty they indicated in his hearers. The Israelites had forgotten God's divine holiness and majesty. Cut loose from this foundation, they were a bewildered people floundering in their relationship to God and in all human relationships as well.

Malachi was sent to arouse the disobedient nation from its spiritual sluggishness and prepare it for the coming of the long-awaited Savior. To that end God gave him this prophecy to thunder out to the people:

"The Lord will suddenly come to His temple. Then I will draw near to you for judgment. From the days of your fathers you have turned aside from My teachings and have not kept them. Now return to Me and I will return to you.

"Return bringing your full tithes into My storehouse, and thereby put Me to the test, and see if I will not open the windows of heaven for you and pour down for you an overflowing blessing."

Then God promised that those who had lived His way would see the end result of their faith: "And I will prepare a book of remembrance of all those who love My name. They shall be Mine, My special possession on the day when I judge, and I will spare them as a man spares his son who serves him. Then you will no more be able to say, 'What is the good of our serving God when evildoers prosper more than we do?'

"For the day is coming when the arrogant and the evildoers shall be as stubble in a burning oven. There will be left of them neither root nor branch. But for you who fear My name, the Sun of Righteousness shall rise with healing in His wings."

And here, in foretelling the coming of Christ, Malachi ended the message God had given him for the people.

And so, to the doubting saints, to the indifferent priests, and to the spiritually careless people as a whole, came Malachi's ringing message from God: "Return to Me and I will return to you, and I will open the windows of heaven and pour down for you an overflowing blessing."

And thus ends the last book of the Old Testament, with the windows of heaven ready to open.

Malachi

CHAPTER 1

HERE IS THE LORD'S MESSAGE TO ISRAEL, given through the prophet Malachi:

2-4 "I have loved you very deeply," says the Lord. But you retort, "Really? When was this?" And the Lord replies, "I showed My love for you by loving your father, Jacob. I didn't need to. I even rejected his very own brother, Esau, and destroyed Esau's mountains and inheritance, to give it to the jackals of the desert. And if his descendants should say, 'We will rebuild the ruins,' then the Lord of Hosts will say, 'Try to if you like, but I will destroy it again,' for their country is named 'The Land of Wickedness' and their people are called "Those Whom God Does Not Forgive.'"

5-6 O Israel, lift your eyes to see what God is doing all around the world; then you will say, "Truly, the Lord's great power goes far beyond our borders!" "A son honors his father, a servant honors his master. I am your Father and Master, yet you don't honor Me, O priests, but you despise My Name."

"Who? Us?" you say. "When did we ever despise Your Name?"

7-9 "When you offer polluted sacrifices on My altar." "Polluted sacrifices? When have we ever done a thing like that?"

"Every time you say, 'Don't bother bringing anything very valuable to offer to God!' You tell the people, 'Lame animals are all right to offer on the altar of the Lord—yes, even the sick and the blind ones.' And you claim this isn't evil? Try it on your governor sometime—give him gifts like that—and see how pleased he is! 'God have mercy on us,' you recite; 'God be gracious to us!' But when you bring that kind of gift, why should He show you any favor at all?

10 "Oh, to find one priest among you who would shut the doors and refuse this kind of sacrifice. I have no pleasure in you," says the Lord of Hosts, "and I will not accept your offerings.

11 "But My Name will be honored by the Gentiles from morning till night. All around the world they will offer sweet

129

incense and pure offerings in honor of My Name. For My Name shall be great among the nations," says the Lord of Hosts.

12 "But you dishonor it, saying that My altar is not important, and encouraging people to bring cheap, sick animals to offer to Me on it.

13-14 "You say, 'Oh, it's too difficult to serve the Lord and do what He asks.' And you turn up your noses at the rules He has given you to obey. Think of it! Stolen animals, lame and sick—as offerings to God! Should I accept such offerings as these?" asks the Lord. "Cursed is that man who promises a fine ram from his flock, and substitutes a sick one to sacrifice to God. For I am a Great King," says the Lord of Hosts, "and My Name is to be mightily revered among the Gentiles."

CHAPTER 2

LISTEN, YOU PRIESTS, to this warning from the Lord of Hosts:

1-3 "If you don't change your ways and give glory to My name, then I will send terrible punishment upon you, and instead of giving you blessings as I would like to, I will turn on you with curses. Indeed, I have cursed you already because you haven't taken seriously the things that are most important to Me. Take note that I will rebuke your children and I will spread on your faces the manure of these animals you offer Me, and throw you out like dung.

4-9 "Then at last you will know it was I who sent you this warning to return to the laws I gave your father Levi," says the Lord of Hosts. "The purpose of these laws was to give him life and peace, to be a means of showing his respect and awe for Me, by keeping them. He passed on to the people all the truth he got from Me. He did not lie or cheat; he walked with Me, living a good and righteous life, and turned many from their lives of sin. Priests' lips should flow with the knowledge of God so the people will learn God's laws. The priests are the messengers of the Lord of Hosts, and men should come to them for guidance. But not to you! For you have left God's paths. Your 'guidance' has caused many to stumble in sin. You have distorted the covenant of Levi, and made it into a grotesque parody," says the Lord of Hosts. "Therefore I have made you contemptible in the eyes of all the

130

people: for you have not obeyed Me, but you let your favorites break the law without rebuke."

10-12 We are children of the same father, Abraham, all created by the same God. And yet we are faithless to each other, violating the covenant of our fathers! In Judah, in Israel and in Jerusalem, there is treachery; for the men of Judah have defiled God's holy and beloved temple by marrying heathen women who worship idols. May the Lord cut off from His covenant every last man, whether priest or layman, who has done this thing!

13 Yet you cover the altar with your tears because the Lord doesn't pay attention to your offerings anymore, and you receive no blessing from Him.

14-16 "Why has God abandoned us?" you cry. I'll tell you why: *it is because the Lord has seen your treachery in divorcing your wives who have been faithful to you through the years, the companions you promised to care for and keep.* You were united to your wife by the Lord. In God's wise plan, when you married, the two of you became one person in His sight. And what does He want? Godly children from your union. Therefore guard your passions! Keep faith with the wife of your youth. For the Lord, the God of Israel, says He hates divorce and cruel men. Therefore control your passions—let there be no divorcing of your wives.

17 You have wearied the Lord with your words. "Wearied Him?" you ask in fake surprise. "How have we wearied Him?"

"By saying that evil is good, that it pleases the Lord! or by saying that God won't punish us—He doesn't care."

CHAPTER 3

LISTEN: I WILL SEND MY MESSENGER before Me to prepare the way. And then the One[1] you are looking for will come suddenly to His temple—the Messenger of God's promises, to bring you great joy. Yes, He is surely coming," says the Lord of Hosts. "But who can live when He appears? Who can endure His coming? For He is like a blazing fire refining precious metal and He can bleach the dirtiest garments!

3-4 "Like a refiner of silver He will sit and closely watch as the dross is burned away. He will purify the Levites, the ministers of God, refining them like gold or silver, so that they will do their

[1]Literally, "the Lord."

work for God with pure hearts. Then once more the Lord will enjoy the offerings brought to Him by the people of Judah and Jerusalem, as He did before.

5-7 "At that time My punishments will be quick and certain; I will move swiftly against wicked men who trick the innocent, against adulterers, and liars, against all those who cheat their hired hands, or oppress widows and orphans, or defraud strangers, and do not fear Me," says the Lord of Hosts. "For I am the Lord—I do not change. That is why you are not already utterly destroyed (for My mercy endures forever).[2] Though you have scorned My laws from earliest time, yet you may still return to Me," says the Lord of Hosts. "Come and I will forgive you. But you say, 'We have never even gone away!'

8-9 "Will a man rob God? Surely not! And yet you have robbed Me. 'What do you mean? When did we ever rob you?' You have robbed Me of the tithes and offerings due to Me. And so the awesome curse of God is cursing you, for your whole nation has been robbing Me.

10-12 "Bring all the tithes into the storehouse so that there will be food enough in My temple; if you do, I will open up the windows of heaven for you and pour out a blessing so great you won't have room enough to take it in! Try it! Let Me prove it to you! Your crops will be large, for I will guard them from insects and plagues. Your grapes won't shrivel away before they ripen," says the Lord of Hosts. "And all nations will call you blessed, for you will be a land sparkling with happiness. These are the promises of the Lord of Hosts.

13 "Your attitude toward Me has been proud and arrogant," says the Lord.

"But you say, 'What do You mean? What have we said that we shouldn't?'

14-15 "Listen, you have said, 'It is foolish to worship God and to obey Him. What good does it do to obey His laws, and to sorrow and mourn for our sins? From now on, as far as we're concerned, Blessed are the arrogant. For those who do evil shall prosper, and those who dare God to punish them shall get off scot-free.' "

16-18 Then those who feared and loved the Lord spoke often of Him to each other. And He had a Book of Remembrance drawn up in which He recorded the names of those who feared

[2]Implied.

Him and loved to think about Him. "They shall be Mine," says the Lord of Hosts, "in that day when I make up My jewels. And I will spare them as a man spares an obedient and dutiful son. Then you will see the difference between God's treatment of good men and bad, between those who serve Him and those who don't."

CHAPTER 4

WATCH NOW," the Lord of Hosts declares, "the day of judgment is coming, burning like a furnace. The proud and wicked will be burned up like straw; like a tree, they will be consumed—roots and all.

2-4 "But for you who fear My Name, the Sun of Righteousness will rise with healing in His wings. And you will go free, leaping with joy like calves let out to pasture. Then you will tread upon the wicked as ashes underfoot," says the Lord of Hosts. "Remember to obey the laws I gave all Israel through Moses, My servant, on Mount Horeb.

5-6 "See, I will send you another prophet like[1] Elijah before the coming of the great and dreadful judgment day of God. His preaching will bring fathers and children together again, to be of one mind and heart, for they will know that if they do not repent, I will come and utterly destroy their land."

[1]Literally, "the prophet Elijah." Compare Matthew 17:10-12 and Luke 1:17.